A History of Free Blacks in America

Lucent Library of Black History

Stuart A. Kallen

LUCENT BOOKS

An imprint of Thomson Gale, a part of The Thomson Corporation

Detroit • New York • San Francisco • San Diego • New Haven, Conn.
Waterville, Maine • London • Munich

THOMSON

GALE

™

© 2006 Thomson Gale, a part of The Thomson Corporation.

Thomson and Star Logo are trademarks and Gale and Lucent Books are registered trademarks used herein under license.

For more information, contact
Lucent Books
27500 Drake Rd.
Farmington Hills, MI 48331-3535
Or you can visit our Internet site at http://www.gale.com

LIBRARY OF CONGRESS CATALOGING-IN-PUBLICATION DATA

Kallen, Stuart A., 1955–
    A history of free Blacks in America / by Stuart Kallen.
        p. c m — (Lucent library of Black history)
    Includes bibliographical references and index.
    ISBN 1-59018-776-8 (lib. bdg. : alk. paper)
    1. Free African Americans—History—Juvenile literature. 2. Free African Americans—Social conditions—Juvenile literature. 3. African Americans—History—To 1863—Juvenile literature. 4. African Americans—Social conditions—To 1964—Juvenile literature. 5. United States—Race relations—Juvenile literature. I. Title. II. Series.
E185.18.K35 2005
973'.0496073—dc22
                                                                                                2005003131

Printed in the United States of America

Contents

Foreword

It has been more than five hundred years since Africans were first brought to the New World in shackles, and over 140 years since slavery was formally abolished in the United States. Over fifty years have passed since the fallacy of "separate but equal" was obliterated in the American courts, and some forty years since the watershed Civil Rights Act of 1965 guaranteed the rights and liberties of all Americans, especially those of color. Over time, these changes have become celebrated landmarks in American history. In the twenty-first century, African American men and women are politicians, judges, diplomats, professors, deans, doctors, artists, athletes, business owners, and home owners. For many, the scars of the past have melted away in the opportunities that have been found in contemporary society. Observers such as Peter N. Kirsanow, who sits on the U.S. Commission of Civil Rights, point to these accomplishments and conclude, "The growing black middle class may be viewed as proof that most of the civil rights battles have been won."

In spite of these legal victories, however, prejudice and inequality have persisted in American society. In 2003, African Americans comprised just 12 percent of the nation's population, yet accounted for 44 percent of its prison inmates and 24 percent of its poor. Racially motivated hate crimes continue to appear on the pages of major newspapers in many American cities. Furthermore, many African Americans still experience either overt or muted racism in their daily lives. A 1996 study undertaken by Professor Nancy Krieger of the Harvard School of Public Health, for example, found that 80 percent of the African American participants reported having experienced racial discrimination in one or more settings, including at work or school, applying for housing and medical care, from the police or in the courts, and on the street or in a public setting.

It is for these reasons that many believe the struggle for racial equality and justice is far from over. These episodes of discrimination threaten to shatter the illusion that America has complete-ly overcome its racist past, causing many black Americans to become increasingly frustrated and confused. Scholar and writer Ellis Cose has described this splintered state in the following way: "I have done everything I was supposed to do. I have stayed out of trouble with the law, gone to the right schools, and worked myself nearly to death. What more do they want? Why in God's name won't they accept me as a full human being?" For Cose and others, the struggle for equality and justice has yet to be fully achieved.

In many subtle yet important ways, the traumatic experiences of slavery and segregation continue to inform the way race is dis-cussed and experienced in the twenty-first century. Indeed, it is possible that America will always grapple with the fallout from its distressing past. Ulric Haynes, dean of the Hofstra University School of Business has said, "Perhaps race will always matter, given the historical circumstances under which we came to this country." But studying this past and understanding how it con-tributes to present-day dialogues about race and history in Amer-ica is a critical component of contemporary education. To this end, the Lucent Library of Black History offers a thorough look at the experiences that have shaped the black community and the American people as a whole. Annotated bibliographies provide readers with ideas for further research, while fully documented primary and secondary source quotations enhance the text. Each book in the series explores a different episode of black history; together they provide students with a wealth of information as well as launching points for further study and discussion.

Free People of Color

In August 1619, European slave traders marched twenty black slaves off a ship in Jamestown, in the present-day state of Virginia. These natives of Africa were the first slaves in North America; by the time the Civil War ended slavery almost 246 years later in 1865, nearly 4 million black slaves lived in the United States. In addition to these millions of men, women, and children who were bought and sold as property, there was a small group of blacks known as free Negroes, free blacks, free people of color, freemen, or simply free people. Although they never made up more than about 2 percent of the nation's population, or 9 percent of all blacks in America, their numbers increased as the population of the United States grew.

Most free people of color were ignored by white society in colonial America, the thirteen colonies ruled by England between the 1600s and 1776. Early in this era, free blacks were allowed to earn wages, accumulate property, hold minor government positions, and even own slaves themselves. One free black man, John Johnson, owned 550 acres in Virginia and worked the land with dozens of slaves.

Freedom was not long unrestricted, however. Limitations of the activities of free blacks began in 1660, when laws governing slavery were written into the Virginia legal code. One law stated that free Negroes "ought not in all respects be admitted to a full fruition of the exemptions and impunities of the English."[1] In plain language this meant that free blacks did not have the same rights as whites. Virginia's lawmakers feared that slaves would rebel against their masters if they believed that once free they could live equally with whites, and worked to discourage such hopes as the economic importance of black slavery grew in the South during the eighteenth century.

Laws were passed that barred free people of color from holding office, voting, serving in the militia, testifying against whites in court, or marrying whites. Free blacks were also given special burdens, such as being forced to pay higher taxes or being punished more severely than whites for criminal acts. Educator and inventor Booker T. Washington, in *The Story of the Negro, Volume 1*, described the situation for free blacks, who were caught between the worlds of whites and slaves: "Under the conditions of slavery, the position of the free Negro was a very uncomfortable one. He was, in a certain sense, an anomaly, since he did not belong to either class. He was distrusted by the white people, and

In this eighteenth-century engraving, the first slaves in North America are brought to shore in Jamestown, Virginia, in 1619.

looked down upon by the slaves [who resented his freedom]."[2]

In the 1770s, conditions began to change slightly for some blacks as Americans spoke passionately of independence and freedom from British rule. In 1776 Thomas Jefferson proclaimed in the Declaration of Independence that "all men are created equal, that they are endowed by their Creator with certain unalienable Rights, that among these are Life, Liberty and the pursuit of Happiness." Inspired by such words, governments in many northern states passed laws to free the slaves within their borders. By the end of the Revolutionary War in 1783, slavery was abolished in Pennsylvania, Vermont, Massachusetts, Connecticut, New York, and New Jersey, and a new population of free blacks was created.

Although most blacks in the South remained locked in the bonds of slavery, the numbers of free blacks overall began to grow rapidly. In 1790 there were about sixty thousand free blacks in the United States. By the 1860s, that number was roughly half a million free people of African descent.

Three Separate Regions

The roles free blacks played in American society differed depending on the region in which they lived. In the early nineteenth century there were three distinct groups of free blacks: those in the North, or free states; those in the slave states of the Upper South; and those in what was known as the Lower South, where the institution of slavery was deeply entrenched. (The western United States was inhabited largely by Native Americans until the mid-1800s, and the black population there was negligible.) Each group of free blacks had unique social, cultural, and economic characteristics.

In the North, blacks made up only about 2 percent of the population in 1790. Their freedom was an inspiration to slaves in the southern states, however, and those who could escape slavery often ran away to Massachusetts, New York, Pennsylvania, Ohio, New Jersey, and other northern states. This swelled the ranks of free blacks in the North. By 1860 about a quarter of a million blacks, slightly less than half of the nation's free people of color, lived above what was known as the Mason-Dixon Line, the surveyor's line that unofficially separated the North from the South.

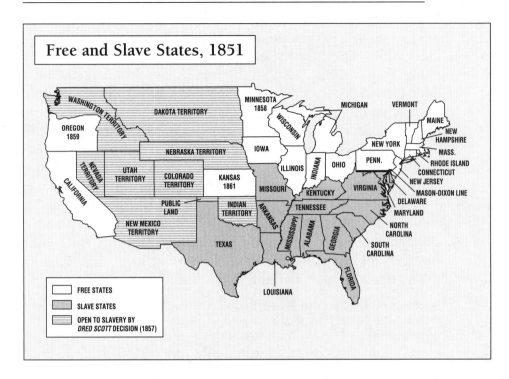

Free and Slave States, 1851

The lives of most free blacks in the North, however, were little changed after emancipation. They were often pushed into the poorest neighborhoods, unemployed or forced to work as unskilled laborers for little pay, and subjected to constant discrimination and prejudice. As Ira Berlin writes in *Slaves Without Masters*:

> Once free, blacks generally remained at the bottom of the social order, despised by whites, burdened with increasingly oppressive racial proscriptions, and subjected to verbal and physical abuse. Free Negroes stood outside the direct governance of a master, but in the eyes of many whites their place in society had not been significantly altered. They were slaves without masters.[3]

Nevertheless, northern blacks enjoyed certain rights that were denied to free blacks elsewhere. They were allowed to travel freely, publish newspapers, hold public meetings and protests, and petition the government in court. Free blacks exercised these rights to speak out and organize against southern slavery.

Free Blacks in the Upper South

As in the North, the ideals of the American Revolution inspired free blacks in the Upper South states of Maryland, Virginia, Kentucky, and Tennessee. But here reforms affected few blacks since slaves made up a much larger percentage of the population. For example, in 1830 there were about 470,000 slaves in Virginia and about 690,000 whites. With slaves making up more than 40 percent of the population, it was in the best interests of the slave owners to limit opportunities for political activism by free people of color. In this atmosphere, whites passed laws that barred blacks from voting, traveling without permission, and meeting without white supervision. Few black newspapers were published, and African American churches, schools, and fraternal societies were often forced to meet in secret.

Slaves serve dinner to a well-to-do Southern family in this illustration from the 1830s. Slaves comprised a large percentage of the populations of several Southern states.

The lack of political opportunities led many free blacks in the Upper South to focus their energies on working and making money. Unlike in the North, where blacks and European immigrants competed for jobs, free black laborers were in demand in the Upper South; thus they enjoyed higher economic status than those in the free states. This attracted free blacks from elsewhere. By the 1810s, the Upper South contained about 120,000 free people of color, who made up about 8 percent of the black population in the region and almost 60 percent of free blacks in the United States at the time. However, repressive laws and an influx of European immigrants, who took most of the jobs, forced many free blacks in the Upper South to move north beginning around 1835.

The Lower South

In the Lower South, where slavery held the tightest grip on the black population, there were few free people of color. South Carolina, Georgia, Alabama, Mississippi, and Louisiana were economically dependent on large numbers of slaves farming labor-intensive crops such as cotton, sugarcane, and tobacco. In most of these states blacks far outnumbered whites, and many slave owners enforced strict measures to prevent slave insurrections. In this rural environment, few blacks were able to gain their freedom. Most free people of color lived in port cities such as Charleston, South Carolina; Mobile, Alabama; and New Orleans, Louisiana.

Most free blacks in the Lower South were descendants of a small group of privileged slaves who were freed by their owners. Many had been house slaves who worked in close contact with white families as nannies, cooks, butlers, and maids. Some were mulattos, the mixed-race children of white slaveholders and black slaves. As a result, more free blacks in the urban South were light skinned. These urban free people of color were also far more skilled than free blacks elsewhere in the United States. For example, in Charleston, over three-quarters of freemen practiced skilled trades such as carpentry.

Wherever free blacks lived, their lives were marked by institutional discrimination and racism. In the years between the American Revolution and the Civil War, free blacks were a small minority in a white society that condoned and exploited slavery. However, as Washington writes:

11

Notwithstanding the hardships and difficulties under which the free Negro population labored, both in the North and in the South, those who had an occasion to study [history] have found that the number of Negroes who had succeeded in making some impression upon their community, either by their native qualities or by their success in business, was more considerable than usually imagined.[4]

Though historians have paid less attention to free blacks in comparison with slaves, many of their stories and contributions to history are noteworthy. These were people who were willing to stand up against racism, discrimination, and the inhumane institution of slavery. They did so in the belief that they were created equal and that, no matter what the price, it was better to seek life, liberty, and the pursuit of happiness than to be bound in servitude and live as the property of another person.

Chapter One

Free Blacks in the Countryside

In the years before the Civil War, the United States was a largely rural society where about 90 percent of the people earned their living from agriculture. Whether farmers were black or white, for the majority who did not own slaves it was a tedious life that required work from sunup to sundown. There were crops to plant, weeds to hoe, fences to build, animals to slaughter, and dozens of other difficult tasks to complete. Men worked in fields, made tools, cared for animals, cut trees for lumber and firewood, hunted, and performed most of the outdoor labor. Women cared for children, cooked, cleaned, and made most household items, including soap, candles, preserves, clothing, and bedding.

Free blacks living in the countryside had additional hardships. Many were former slaves who had been manumitted, or set free, by slave owners. Though freedom was considered a great gift, few free blacks had enough money to purchase land of their own. As a result, many labored as hired hands on farms owned by whites. In the South, this often meant that free blacks worked side by side with slaves in the fields. They were hired only at certain times of the year when extra hands were needed to plant or harvest, and they were paid a pittance for their work. While they

Two free black women on a plantation in Mississippi wash clothes while the children of the family relax with their grandfather on the porch of a former slave shack.

may have been free, they were treated like slaves by their employers.

Farming was not the only labor available in the countryside. Free blacks also built roads, dug ditches, and worked in forests. Oftentimes freemen were hired to perform jobs such as logging. Such jobs were considered too dangerous for valuable slaves, who could cost up to $2,000 apiece, a fortune at the time.

Free blacks were restricted in other ways. In most southern states free people of color had to register with county courts and prove that they were free, not runaway slaves. If they could do so to the satisfaction of authorities, the freemen were issued certificates that allowed them to remain free. If they could not, the applicant could be jailed and sold into slavery at a public auction. Even with a certificate proving his freedom, the freeman was not allowed to travel to another county in search of employment without a special permit that cost several dollars, too much for most low-wage earners. This effectively locked rural free blacks into one place.

Despite these hardships, some free blacks managed to thrive while their neighbors simply survived. The quality of life for rural free blacks often depended on the region they lived in, the local economy, and local whites' attitudes about slavery and ex-slaves.

Emancipation in Virginia

Except for a few areas of Rhode Island, the Hudson Valley, and southern New Jersey, free blacks in the Northeast lived mostly in urban areas. In the Upper South, however, where farming was more central to the economy, there are more records of free blacks living in the countryside. In Virginia, for example, the

Free Blacks as Slave Owners

Government documents indicate that some free blacks owned slaves themselves. The reasons for this arrangement sometimes had to do with the peculiarity of the legal system. In Virginia after 1806, for example, it was illegal for free blacks to stay in the state longer than twelve months after they had been emancipated. Those who had been freed before the law went into effect sometimes purchased the freedom of their mates, children, friends, and relatives. Since these people could not be freed without leaving the state, for legal purposes they were kept as slaves by free blacks. This created an unusual situation where husbands owned their wives or wives owned their husbands and offspring. Of course, some freed blacks used slaves as forced labor, as Ira Berlin notes in *Slaves Without Masters*:

> Economic success in the South depended largely on the ownership of slaves, and free Negroes were no more exempt from this than whites. Although most free Negro slaveholders were truly benevolent despots, owning only their families and friends to prevent their enslavement or forcible deportation, a small minority of wealthy freemen exploited slaves for commercial purposes. This small group of free Negroes were generally the wealthiest and best-connected members of their caste.

numbers of free blacks began to grow in 1782, a year before the end of the Revolutionary War. This was largely due to the influence of Thomas Jefferson, who, as governor of Virginia, signed a bill that legalized manumission. This law allowed slaveholders to make promises in their wills to emancipate their slaves upon the owners' deaths. Hundreds of slaveholders followed suit, and more than ten thousand slaves were freed by 1790, with another ten thousand manumitted by 1800. Some of the more fortunate freedmen, as they were called, were also granted small parcels of land, farm implements, and other benefits to help them attain self-sufficiency. For example, in 1803 unmarried planter William Ludwell Lee of Green Spring, Virginia, wrote in his will that all his slaves were to be emancipated:

In his will, Virginia planter John Randolph bequeathed money to his freed slaves to help them buy land in Ohio.

[The adults] may be allowed to settle on such parts of my . . . lands as my executors may designate, where I wish comfortable houses to be built for them . . . a sufficiency of Indian corn allowed . . . for one year . . . [and] for ten years [they may live] free of any rent.[5]

Virginia's experiment with manumission was short-lived, however. Many slave owners were vehemently opposed to the law, claiming that the existence of free blacks depreciated the value of their slaves and inspired those who remained slaves to run away. Slave owners prevailed, and the manumission law was repealed in 1806. Any slaves who were freed after that date were required to leave the state within twelve months or be returned to slavery. This created an influx of free people of color in new settlements in rural Ohio, Indiana, Michigan, and Illinois, regions that had recently become states.

In rare instances, entire communities were created overnight. For example, when Virginian Samuel Gist died in 1819, his will ordered the emancipation of his 113 slaves. He delegated his trustees to purchase a large parcel of land in Ohio for the freed people to farm. That same year Edward Coles, a friend of Jefferson, purchased 160 acres of land for each of his 100 slaves.

As increasing numbers of white pioneers populated Ohio and other states, a movement grew to prevent the settlement of free blacks. In 1826 Virginia planter John Randolph left $13,000 to purchase thirty-two hundred acres of Ohio land for his four hundred slaves. When the free blacks arrived, according to a newspaper article quoted in *The Negro in Virginia*, they were "forcibly prevented from making settlement. . . . Since then acts of hostility have been commenced against the people of the settlement and threats of greater force held out if they do not abandon their lands and homes."[6] The freed people persevered, however, and the descendants of those settlers are still living in that part of Ohio.

"Capable of Taking Care of Themselves"

Hundreds of free blacks also made their way to Indiana. Some were emancipated in Virginia; others had been able to earn enough money to purchase their freedom. One such group of eleven black families began farming the area around Madison in the 1820s. Emma Lou Thornbrough describes the situation in *The Negro in Indiana*:

They had cleared land and become successful farmers, growing wheat, rye, hemp, and a little tobacco. [A man] named Crosby had come from Kentucky thirteen years before and had since acquired two small farms, totaling 137 acres. He had cleared about one fourth of the land and was the owner of six cows, four horses, and other farm animals. A neighbor was Fountain Thurman, a man of unusual intellect and skill, who had mastered several trades, including those of mason, well digger, and rock blaster while yet a slave. He had been able to persuade his master to let him buy his freedom by earning money at his various trades. The master agreed, on the terms that Thurman should pay him one hundred dollars a year for seven years. In the seven years the slave was able to earn not only the money to purchase his own freedom but enough besides to redeem his wife and children from slavery. He came to Jefferson County, where he bought an eighty-acre farm at three dollars an acre. As the result of the improvements he made on it, he was later offered seven hundred dollars for the land.[7]

Many of Crosby and Thurman's colleagues were also former slaves from farther south. Turner Newsom, for example, migrated from North Carolina to Rush County, Indiana, southeast of present-day Indianapolis, with only thirty-seven cents. By taking whatever work he could find, Newsom acquired, cleared, drained, and then developed his land. When Newsom died in 1850, he left his family a 160-acre farm, a two-story house, a barn, and a stylish two-horse carriage.

Such stories were typical. By the 1850s, eighty-one families of free blacks lived in the Spiceland region, about forty miles east of Indianapolis. Collectively they owned more than three thousand acres worth $105,000. The farmers were even able to pay the expensive tuition to send their children to private schools. Such success stories were celebrated by white abolitionists, activists who advocated the abolition of slavery. In 1842 the abolitionist newspaper *Free Labor Advocate* described the success of ex-slave farmers in the Cabin Creek settlement, northeast of Indianapolis:

> It seems to me that no reasonable person could visit this settlement, become acquainted with the situation and character of the inhabitants and witness the improvements many of them are making and not be an abolitionist! At any rate he would be satisfied that [free blacks] are capable of taking care of themselves if they have anything like a fair chance.[8]

Unfortunately, there were those who worked to deny free black farmers their fair chance for success. When Virginia planter

Considered a Slave
Until Proven Otherwise

In Mississippi in 1850 there were nearly 310,000 slaves and fewer than 1,500 free blacks. Despised by slave owners, free blacks had to fight to maintain their status. Charles S. Sydnor describes the situation in *Free Blacks in America, 1800–1860* (edited by Bracey et al.).

> [Free blacks] received much attention from the white people—attention that was usually hostile. . . . Probably the key to the condition of the free negro and mulatto can be found in the assumption that all [people of color] were considered slaves unless the contrary could be proved. . . . Every free negro was required to present himself at court, county or probate, and give evidence of his non-servile condition. If the proof was satisfactory the court would have the negro supplied with a certified copy of the record. This certificate would show the name, color, stature, and any distinguishing features or scars of the recipient, and this bit of parchment was all that stood between the free negro and many possible troubles. The certificate had to be renewed every three years and each time there was a fee of one dollar—in 1831 increased to three dollars. . . . As for the negro who could not produce his registered bit of paper or parchment, there was the danger of being seized by some unscrupulous white person and either held or sold as a slave. Any alleged free negro who did not possess a certificate might be jailed, and upon failure to establish his freedom in a certain length of time the law required his sale at public auction.

John Warwick bequeathed a large parcel of land in Indiana to seventy-four of his slaves in 1848, Indiana officials passed a law banning the immigration of free blacks. However, the rural character of the state at the time meant that such laws were difficult, if not impossible, to enforce, and ex-slaves continued to move to Indiana to fulfill their dreams of freedom.

"A Degree of Autonomy"

Although they faced discrimination, rural free blacks in states such as Indiana lived much better than those freemen who remained in the South, where they were greatly outnumbered by slaves and whites. For example, in 1810 there were only 1,800 free blacks in Georgia, about 4,000 in South Carolina, and only 240 in Mississippi. While most lived in port cities, those who resided in rural areas often lived in secluded parts of the countryside in ramshackle cabins and shanties on parcels of land that no one else wanted. Usually far away from major roads, sometimes these settlements grew into small villages whose residents preferred to remain isolated, unknown, and undiscovered, as Berlin explains: "These . . . villages, however ramshackle, allowed free Negroes a degree of autonomy and a chance to escape the pressures of the white-dominated world."[9]

Far from slave owners and government officials, some were able to avoid the high taxes governments levied on freemen. In 1828 a frustrated South Carolina sheriff was appointed the task of collecting back taxes from delinquent free blacks living in an isolated forest. However, the sheriff complained about "the difficulties in finding them, on account of their part peculiar situation of their place of residence."[10]

The Laboring Population

Most free people of color in the rural South did not acquire the independence necessary to avoid sheriffs and tax collectors. In fact, many were forced to live on land owned by the people for whom they worked. For example, in Virginia in 1830 nearly one-half of the state's forty-seven thousand free blacks lived with their white employers. In North Carolina, so many blacks lived with their bosses that state law required white employers to collect the taxes of free blacks living in their households. Many white employers were slave owners who treated the free blacks just as they did their slaves. Freemen lived in broken-down slave quarters, harvested crops, performed seasonal work, hunted for their employers, and fished on boats piloted by white riverboat captains.

Unlike the slaves with whom they worked, free black farm laborers were paid for their labors—but paid poorly. In North Carolina a farmhand could expect to earn less than $10 a month at a time when a white carpenter might earn about four times as much. Free blacks nonetheless played an important role in southern agriculture, as one unnamed Maryland lawmaker stated: "It is unquestionable . . . that quite a large part of our soil would not be tilled without their aid."[11]

The situation for free black women working on farms was slightly better. Although they were paid less than field hands, the work they performed was less strenuous. Most worked indoors as cooks, maids, and servants. North Carolina cooks could earn about $75 a year, while a house servant might earn about $80.

Many farmhands worked for white farmers who owned small parcels of land and could not afford to purchase slaves. As the *Richmond Whig* newspaper in Virginia noted in 1858, there were "many families in the state . . . whose condition is such that they cannot afford the luxury of a servant, at the present high rates of hire, but who are in the habit of hiring free Negroes, for one or two days a week, to perform those offices for which a slave is indispensable."[12]

A family of tenant farmers tends to chores outside their log cabin. Most plantation owners housed their free black farmhands in dilapidated slave quarters.

By the 1850s, slavery in the United States was a deeply divisive issue. Free black communities in the Upper South suffered as slaveholders became more adamant in their opposition to free people of color living in their communities. This was especially true in Virginia, where proslavery politicians tried to pass laws to expel the state's fifty thousand free blacks. In northern Virginia, however, there was a labor shortage that was eased by the presence of free blacks. An editorial in the *Richmond Inquirer* addressed this issue in 1845:

Shall she [Virginia] at such a time suddenly expel from her borders 50,000 of her laboring population and that to when the very demand for labor and increased wages are operating to improve the condition and character of those

Tenant farmers pick bales of cotton on a Georgia plantation. As tenant farmers, they were entitled to a small portion of the cotton harvest.

whom it is proposed to expel? The people living in the sections where the free Negro population [are] largest . . . [are] not clamoring for the bill to expel this class. Such people [are] most willing to retain them.[13]

Other newspapers in the area speculated that the eviction of the free blacks would cause economic ruin to tobacco planters in the areas where most black farm laborers lived. This would be particularly true during harvest time when tobacco had to be harvested, gathered, and treated in a timely fashion.

Tenant Farmers

Although free black farm laborers were in great demand in Virginia, they were paid much less there than elsewhere. They were given food and clothing and a nominal wage of about $20 to $40 per year. Some white farmers also allowed free black farm laborers to work a small portion of the farm for themselves as compensation. The farmer might lend the laborer farm implements, seed, and other necessities and allow the employee to plant twenty-five or more acres for himself.

Black farmhands could also bargain with white landholders to work a section of land and then pay the farmer back with harvested crops or livestock in the fall. Free black farmers typically bargained with merchants to obtain seed stock, tools, and other necessities. These loans were repaid with money, crops, or livestock. For example, records show that a tenant farmer named John Tate owed a local merchant $44.69. In return, Tate offered two oxen and a portion of his cultivated crop of wheat then growing on the land of a local landholder.

In some cases tenant farmers eventually earned enough money to become independent farmers themselves. For instance, records from 1830 in Isle of Wight County, Virginia, show that free black tenant farmer Burwell Green farmed rented land. Twelve years later, county records show that Green owned sixty-three acres.

A few freemen were able to parlay landownership status into considerable wealth. For example, William Epps of Halifax County, Virginia, owned only one horse in 1830. By successfully farming rented acreage he was able to acquire land, and he owned nearly six hundred acres by 1842. During that time Epps purchased equipment worth $2,966, a veritable fortune at a time when a farm laborer was paid $20 per year.

Similar success stories were uncommon, however. A majority of free blacks labored for others or worked on tenant farms. In Virginia, for example, about two out of three free blacks were farm laborers without any claim to land; the other third were either small landowners or tenant farmers.

Gloomy and Uninviting Turpentine Towns

Rural freemen could do more than farm. In the eighteenth and nineteenth centuries, one of the primary industries outside of agriculture in the Carolinas and Virginia was the production of turpentine and pitch from pine sap. These substances were as important as petroleum is in modern times. Turpentine was used to produce paints and varnishes, disinfectants, liniments, medicated soaps, internal medicines, ointments, explosives, synthetic rubber, inks, insecticides, crayons, and dozens of other products. Pitch was used like coal in fires and for waterproofing ships, barrels, and other products.

Throughout the forest, slaves, free blacks, and poor whites worked in turpentine camps. The work involved slicing large notches in pine trees with axes, attaching wooden boxes to catch the gum, and packing barrels of the gooey substance on the backs of mules for transportation to turpentine distilleries. The work was labor intensive and took place in hot, insect- and snake-ridden forests. Judging from the description of a "turpentine town" near present-day Horry, South Carolina, by local resident J.W. Ogilvie, those who engaged in the work, both black and white, did not enjoy a pleasant life:

> For the most part the habitations of the populace were crude log cabins with mud chimneys generally backing the road as if they were gruesome sentinels placed there to challenge the entrance of improvement and progress. The surroundings were primeval in their confusion, and in many, yea very many, instances the commonest and rudest comforts of life were almost unknown. Their environments were gloomy and uninviting. They seemed to be a people without hope in the future and concerned only about their

Free blacks load barrels of turpentine onto a wagon at a distillery in Wilmington, North Carolina. Workers at such distilleries performed backbreaking labor for very poor wages.

present needs and necessities. Seemingly their ambition lie[s] in scraping a pine tree.[14]

The town described by Ogilvie was undoubtedly owned by a company that employed the workers. Though the employers housed workers in these bleak cabins, they did not pay their help. Instead, workers were given tokens that could be exchanged at the company store for groceries, liquor, and other needs. Ogilvie described this form of exchange:

The circulating medium was almost exclusively a piece of round or square cardboard bearing the information that it was good for such and such an amount in trade at so and so, and further that this was not transferable. These bits of cardboard represented the price of labor. They were the shackles that bound the people. The laborer was even denied the privilege of spending the fruits of his labor in a manner and in such a way that to him seemeth best in contributing toward the comfort, happiness and pleasure of himself and family.[15]

Fleeing the Countryside

Those who remained on farms and in forest settlements usually had little hope of advancement or acceptance. Harsh, unrelenting

Free Black Women

Free women of color who lived in the countryside most often performed the tasks of typical farm wives, raising children, milking cows, tending chickens and pigs, growing vegetable gardens, and selling their produce. Those who raised sheep supplemented their income by spinning wool, weaving it into cloth, and sewing it into clothing. John Hope Franklin explains in *The Free Negro in North Carolina, 1790–1860.*

> There were few skilled occupations which free Negro women could enter. The most important were those of spinning, weaving, and dressmaking. The number of free Negro girls who were apprenticed in these fields suggests that a sizable number would be capable of engaging in these occupations upon coming of age. Catherine Stanly augmented the financial resources which her father left her by making dresses for white women. . . . A number of free Negro women increased the family income by spinning and weaving the clothes for their own family and for others. In 1860, there were almost 300 free Negro spinners and weavers in North Carolina, of whom women comprised a considerable majority. At the same time, 175 free Negro women were engaged in the occupation of dressmaking. Free Negro women also secured considerable employment as midwives and nurses. Here and there, free Negro women branched out into other lines. For example, Mary A. Lee conducted a profitable bakery shop in . . . Washington County, and in 1860 she was worth $2,750.

work and white prejudice led many free blacks to leave the countryside for the imagined ease of city life. There, free black communities offered employment, housing, cultural events, and a buffer against grinding racism. As a result, between 1790 and 1820, a steady stream of workers left the rural South for coastal and northern cities.

Chapter Two

Working in the City

The story of free blacks in America between the Revolutionary War and the Civil War is most often written in the histories of major cities such as New York, Philadelphia, Boston, Baltimore, Charleston, Norfolk, and New Orleans. In these population centers free people of color sought a better life than that available to them in the countryside. The statistics tell this story. For example, while the free black population in Virginia doubled between 1790 and 1810, the free black population of Richmond increased 400 percent and that of Norfolk grew tenfold. Baltimore had the most spectacular growth during that two-decade period, as the population grew from three hundred free people of color to five thousand. In later years growth was even more dramatic as most of America's largest cities filled with escaped and manumitted slaves, former country dwellers, and freeborn people of color.

In short, cities offered free blacks opportunity and community. By the 1820s nearly every good-sized city had at least one African American church that operated independently from white religious institutions. Cities also had schools organized for blacks, charity organizations and benevolent societies, grocery stores that catered to black tastes, and taverns, entertainment

A group of free blacks looking for work arrives in St. Louis, Missouri. Northern cities provided free blacks with work opportunities unavailable in the South.

venues, and other institutions that were independent and free of control from white society.

City Life in the North

Though northern states abolished slavery at the end of the American Revolution, slavery faded gradually. For example, in 1820 there were twenty thousand slaves in the North and a population of nearly 100,000 free blacks. By 1840, however, the number of northern slaves fell to less than a thousand, with a free black population of more than 171,000. By 1860, slavery was nonexistent among the quarter-million free blacks living in urban areas of the North.

Freedom in the North naturally attracted many emancipated southern slaves, as well as runaways who migrated to cities to get as far away from bondage as possible. Thus, southern accents were common among the African Americans in Chicago, where

nearly half the free black population had been born in the South. About a third of the free people of color in Philadelphia were born in the South, as were about 25 percent of Boston's free blacks. This large-scale migration brought white backlash, as Ira Berlin notes:

In the North, blacks were [as] despised and degraded as in the South. Whites usually proscribed them from political rights, barred them from most public institutions, segregated them in others, and limited them to the most menial jobs in the worst housing. . . . [Many] blacks saw little to distinguish the racism of the North from that of the South.[16]

"The Bottom of the Social Order"

Free blacks in the cities of the North faced other obstacles. Many, having worked only as farm laborers, possessed few skills necessary to survive in the competitive urban job market. They had no guarantees of schooling, career training, or job placement to offset minimal job prospects.

Nor were former slaves given reparations for their years of suffering or sympathy for their disadvantages. As Berlin notes,

Northern whites believe that those who enjoyed liberty, worked hard, were clever enough and lucky enough would prosper. Those who did not, should not—and with justice. So when the largely unskilled blacks, many without experience in the free marketplace, fell to the bottom of the social order, many whites believed they knew the reason why: Blacks were lazy, stupid, and corrupt. . . . But the newly freed blacks did not merely fall in occupational standing—whites anxious to confirm their cherished racial ideals frequently pushed them down.[17]

Free blacks who were skilled artisans fared little better. Experienced ex-slave cabinetmakers, candle makers, tailors, coopers (barrel makers), and other craftsmen could not find work in their former trades because white bosses would not hire them and white employees would not work beside them. Unable to assimilate in the workplace, free blacks were mostly hired to perform menial jobs no matter what their experience. Scottish travel writer John M. Duncan lamented the plight of free blacks in *Travels Through Part of the United States and Canada in 1818 and 1819:* "Chains of a stronger kind still manacled their limbs, for which no legislative act could free them; a mental and moral subordination and inferiority, to which tyrant custom has here subjected all the sons and daughters of Africa."[18]

Free blacks' dreams of steady employment, which Berlin notes would afford "family stability, religious freedom, political independence, and social mobility,"[19] faded even further when in the 1840s millions of white immigrants from Ireland and Germany began flocking to northern cities. White employers much preferred to hire these newly arrived immigrants for both low-paying positions and skilled trades. In *Free Blacks in America, 1800–1860,* editors John H. Bracey Jr., August Meier, and Elliot Rudwick describe the situation:

> [During] the course of the nineteenth century, the position of the black artisan-entrepreneur deteriorated. As the white working class grew in numbers . . . its members made determined efforts to exclude blacks from the better-paying occupations. . . . [In] the Northern states, the arrival of nearly five million white immigrants . . . posed an alarming threat to the Negroes' already meager employment opportunities. Gradually many blacks were displaced by immigrants, especially the Irish, as longshoremen and railroad workers, [bricklayers], waiters, barbers, and even porters and bootblacks, while Negro women began losing positions as maids, cooks, and washerwomen. On the waterfront,

Petitioning for Freedom

———◆———

In Massachusetts, where the American Revolution was born, slaves began petitioning courts for their freedom almost as soon as legal disputes erupted between Americans and the British in the 1760s. In 1766 an unnamed black woman in Massachusetts sued for her freedom while founding father and future president John Adams looked on in the courtroom.

In January 1773, hoping to gain freedom for those held in bondage in Massachusetts, a group of slaves including Peter Petion, Sambo Freeman, and Felix Holbrook petitioned the general court of the state legislature for their freedom. In an emotional plea, reprinted in Benjamin Quarles's *The Negro in the American Revolution*, the men wrote that their legal status as slaves deprived them of family and nation, saying, "We have no property! we have no wives! we have no children! no city! no country!" When the legislature failed to act, the men went to the office of governor Tom Hutchinson, who claimed he could not help them. In May 1774 the group sent another petition to the legislature, but were ignored. Six weeks later they again asked for their freedom and also asked for small parcels of land, according to the petition, so that "each of us may there sit down quietly under his own fig tree." Although the petition was once again denied, by the end of the Revolution, slavery was virtually abolished through legislative process and court actions in Massachusetts, Pennsylvania, Vermont, Connecticut, Rhode Island, New York, and New Jersey.

economic competition and hostility between the two groups was exacerbated when employers, playing one race against the other, hired black workmen as strikebreakers. In New York City this policy produced among the predominantly Irish longshoremen an intense animosity that came to a violent climax in the bloody race riots of 1863.[20]

In this explosive climate, most free black laborers in New York, Philadelphia, Boston, and elsewhere held the lowest-paying jobs. They were porters and errand runners, servants, newsboys,

A flyer printed by the African Society in the 1830s depicts a simple pictorial history of slaves in the United States and calls for the abolition of slavery.

and peddlers. About 10 to 20 percent, however, were able to find better means of employment and worked as printers, bricklayers, stable hands, shoemakers, and factory hands.

Mutual Aid and Charity Organizations

Free blacks in the North nevertheless enjoyed many freedoms unavailable to their southern counterparts. One important difference was the rise in community organizations known as mutual aid societies. One such organization, the African Society, founded in Boston in 1796, had two hundred members by 1810, about one out of every ten free blacks in Boston. Funded by membership dues and donations from wealthier patrons, the society offered welfare for the needy in the form of financial aid and job placement. Widows, orphans, and the disabled were also provided with money, food, clothing, firewood, and other necessities.

The society, in conjunction with the African Baptist Church, also provided for members' religious needs and served as a moral compass, urging its members to adhere to the strict Puritan attitudes prevalent in Boston at that time. For example, the society promised to take care of any widow member only "so long as she behaves herself decently." Drinking to excess was also forbidden, and the rules stated that "any member bringing on himself a sickness or disorder by intemperance, shall not be considered as entitled to any benefits of assistance from the society."[21]

Society members believed that the best way they could combat prejudice was to hold themselves up to the highest moral standards. They often spoke out against gambling, crime, and other vices among free blacks. One crime, however, was encouraged. Although it was illegal to harbor and aid runaway slaves, members of the African Society were "conductors" and "stationmasters" on the Underground Railroad, providing safe houses and passage to Canada for fugitives from the South.

Free blacks who were not members of mutual aid societies could turn to fraternal organizations that offered a wide variety of other diversions. The African Masonic Lodge and the African American Female Intelligence Society, for example, organized musical concerts, lectures, and debates. Churches sponsored choirs and orchestras where vocal training, musical tutoring, and classical music performance opportunities were available. Several times a year, the fraternal organizations sponsored dances and music festivals that were open to the public.

Bars and Gambling Halls

Those who chafed at the propriety of black mutual aid and fraternal societies could socialize in barrooms and gambling halls, which were open to blacks and whites alike. Black seamen, porters, and other laborers faced little prejudice at such places, located usually near docks and shipping warehouses, if they had money to spend. In these seedy establishments men ate raw clams, drank poor-quality liquor, smoked cheap cigars, and were entertained by dancers and prostitutes. Music was often provided by laborers who moonlighted in bands that played the popular tunes of the day. The main entertainment, however, was the so-called sporting event where rats and dogs fought to the death in rat pits while the cheering crowd bet on the prospective winners. As might be expected, the neighborhoods home to such locales were bothersome to many citizens, both black and white. In *Black Bostonians*, James Oliver Horton and Lois E. Horton describe the situation in Boston's notorious North End:

> The North End was an area of particular concern to the Boston police, a constant source of irritation to black temperance reformers, and a challenge to church missionaries.

Excessive drinking was a problem for many in the North End. In April 1855, a black sailor was found dead in his boarding house bed. [According to police reports,] he died of "lung fever" aggravated by alcoholic drink. Often, intoxication was a major contributing factor to crimes of violence, as when James Marshall, "crazy drunk," assaulted James Brown, a fellow laborer, with a hatchet. Drunken quarrels resulting in arrests were not unusual, especially on weekends.[22]

Diverse Occupations in the Cities of the Upper South

By the early 1800s, Charleston and Baltimore were, respectively, the fourth and fifth largest cities in the United States (after Philadelphia, New York, and Boston). Baltimore in particular was considered a boomtown, with a rapidly expanding economy and population. These and other cities in the Upper South attracted many free blacks from the countryside in the early years of the eighteenth century.

Free blacks were in great demand in the expanding labor market. Jobs were plentiful in Richmond, where half of all free blacks worked in tobacco factories, paper mills, and iron foundries. Factory workers spent money in their communities, and their steady employment supported hundreds of self-employed workers such as door-to-door salespersons, gardeners, and clothes washers. In Baltimore, employment opportunities were more diverse, as Christopher Phillips explains in *Freedom's Port:*

The 1817–1818 Baltimore city directory lists 402 "free householders of colour," who engaged collectively in fifty-five different occupations. Though the largest single occupation was laborer, significant numbers of free Negroes also took up such semiskilled trades as carting . . . sawing, driving hacks, coaches, and stages, whitewashing, brickmaking, bricklaying, nailmaking, boot and shoe blacking, brushmaking, harnessmaking, baking, cigarmaking, dyeing, comb making, potting, stonecutting, and gluemaking. Moreover, a number of others acquired enough expertise to engage in such highly skilled trades as blacksmithing, tanning, barbering, coopering [barrel making], shoemaking, carpentry, and butchering. . . . Many of these skilled and semiskilled artisans

The Local Barbershop

—■—

Barbershops in nineteenth-century black urban neighborhoods were more than haircutting salons. As James Oliver Horton and Lois E. Horton write in *Black Bostonians*, barbershops were community centers, social clubs, and even places to hide runaway slaves who were traveling on the Underground Railroad.

> [The] local barber shop was an important forum for the discussion and exchange of political ideas and community information. Peter Howard's barber shop [in Boston], for example, was a gathering place for all segments of black society—for those who were likely to be members of formal [antislavery] protest groups and for those who were not. For many, the underemployed and the barely literate, the conversation at Howard's shop was often the only form of political education available. Job openings were posted in the shop, and community information was available there along with tickets for community events. For over twenty years [between the 1840s and the 1860s] Howard's, located at the foot of Beacon Hill on Cambridge Street, was one of the most popular gathering places in the community.
>
> Although Howard's was well known for its provocative discussions, few outside the community understood the extent of its function—for the shop was an important station on the underground railroad. Through the rear door and the connecting alleys beyond, many fugitives [runaway slaves] who chose to remain in the city for a time joined other blacks who came to the shop for the services of its proprietor and to share in the fellowship of conversation.

managed to open their own stores and shops, while still others without special skills did likewise, running oyster houses, cook shops [diners], and various retail shops.[23]

There were also opportunities in what could loosely be

described as the entertainment business. Entrepreneurs set up in cellars, alleys, and back rooms of grocery stores to offer alcohol, games of chance, and prostitutes to black and white patrons alike. By 1839 these illicit businesses were such a problem to some that the *Baltimore Sun* editorialized that police should "break up the filthy little groggeries, where the most debased and abject of our black . . . population assembles to drink and gamble [and engage in] obscene language and drunken orgies."[24] Despite the complaints, Baltimore police, many of whom were customers of the "groggeries," did little to close them down.

Free black women worked in the typical female trades of the day as domestics, nurses, maids, cooks, and nannies. Many took jobs as laundresses, washing clothes for white customers. This was labor-intensive work, requiring the laundress to carry water, scrub clothes by hand, and hang them out to dry, often in frigid weather. Laundry work had advantages, however, that made up for the backbreaking labor, as Tommy L. Bogger explains in *Free Blacks in Norfolk, Virginia, 1790–1860:*

A woman in Florida washes clothes in an outdoor tub. Many free black women took jobs as laundresses.

Unlike domestics, laundresses were independent business operators whose work was not conducted under the close scrutiny of whites. They worked from their own homes and they set their own schedules. Best of all, laundering was most suited for mothers with young children. They did not have to choose between finding babysitters or leaving the children unattended. Moreover, the children could assist in doing the work and making deliveries. Not much capital was needed to start a laundering business, and some of the women found it to be a profitable enterprise.[25]

Driven to the Wall

As in the North, the labor market for free blacks in the Upper South began to change in the 1840s and 1850s with the influx of Irish and German immigrants. In Baltimore, nearly ten thousand immigrants were arriving every year in the 1850s, and similar increases were seen in other cities in the region as well. For free blacks who were already marginalized, this new competition for low-wage jobs and cheap housing was disastrous. White employers preferred white workers, and many free blacks lost their jobs. Among the wealthy, there was status attached to having white maids, coachmen, butlers, and other domestics, and merchants liked to boast that their household servants were all white. The same held true on the docks and factory floors. As Baltimore attorney John H.B. Latrobe wrote in 1851:

> [Not long ago] the shipping . . . was loaded by freed colored stevedores. The labor at the coal yards was free colored labor . . . . Now all this is changed. [I see] every European arrival as a sign and a warning to free black workers [for as foreigners] enter into competition with the black man in all avenues of labor—in most of them [they] drive him to the wall. . . . The white man stands in the black man's shoes; or else is fast getting into them.[26]

Free People in the Lower South

The poverty experienced by many free blacks in the Upper South was even worse in the Lower South. Most free blacks here were relegated to the least desirable neighborhoods, either located far

In 1863 police are called in to quell a riot that broke out in a densely populated black neighborhood in Harlem, New York.

from the center of town, along flood-prone river plains, next to railroad tracks, or close to polluting paper mills, steel mills, or slaughterhouses. For example, the Oglethorpe area of Savannah, Georgia, where 50 percent of the city's free blacks lived, was between a river and busy railroad tracks in the industrialized part of the city. In the summer the hot, humid air was often thick with black smoke from coal-burning trains, riverboats, and foundries. There were no parks and few open spaces; every block was occupied by warehouses, workshops, slaughterhouses, and railroad yards.

Barred from living in white neighborhoods, free blacks made the best of their situation, living in lofts and cellars on commercial property and building their own apartments in abandoned warehouses and factories with scrap wood, tin, and brick. Margaret Douglass, a white woman who was jailed in the 1850s for teaching black children to read, describes a home she visited in Norfolk, Virginia. Although located in the Upper South region, the condition is indicative of a typical urban dwelling inhabited by the poor:

> [The home] is a tottering hovel, situated in the heart of Norfolk. It is a miserable apology for a human habitation, containing but two [rooms], one above the other. Inside conditions are worse. On one side of the first or ground floor . . . is a wretched bed supported by some boards, and broken chairs.[27]

There were exceptions to the bleak housing situation faced by most free blacks. A few who achieved great wealth were able to live alongside whites in some of the South's better neighborhoods. For example, William Johnson, a successful barber and moneylender in Natchez, Mississippi, lived in a large brick house among the finest homes in that city situated along the Mississippi River.

Home in New Orleans

William Johnson's situation was unusual for free blacks in Mississippi. Farther south in New Orleans, however, free blacks formed a unique society unlike any other in the United States. New Orleans was America's most multicultural city, with slaves, Europeans, Americans, free blacks, and immigrants from the Caribbean living, working, and playing together. In this mix of cultures, the most prominent citizens among the free blacks were light-skinned people called Creoles, people of mixed black and French or Spanish ancestry. An unnamed Spanish bishop complained about this coupling of whites and blacks at the end of the eighteenth century, writing: "The military officers and a good many inhabitants . . . live almost publicly with colored concubines, and they do not blush at carrying the illegitimate [children] that they have by them to be recorded in the parochial registries as their natural children."[28]

Other free blacks in New Orleans were former house slaves who had been manumitted. Although comparatively few in number,

The Economics of Free Black Labor

In the Upper South, plantation owners often rented out their slaves to businesses during winter and other slow times of the year. Many employers, however, preferred to hire free blacks as laborers, as Christopher Phillips explains in *Freedom's Port*.

> Many employers preferred free black men and women to slaves in their households and businesses because they were readily available and less expensive. The free labor system offered employers the flexibility to hire and lay off wage laborers according to the vagaries of the market. As a result, Baltimore industries employed far more free blacks than slaves to maintain elasticity in labor costs. Hiring a slave often involved not only paying the going wage but also feeding, clothing, and being responsible for the health of that slave during the term of contract, as well as making sure that the bond-person did not run off while out of the master's charge. Hiring a free Negro . . . simply involved paying the wage, which made far more sense financially than hiring a slave. Moreover, ambitious employers often wanted more incentive for productive labor than a master's lash—one they often could not wield themselves. As the [nineteenth-century] editor J.D.B. DeBow observed, many capitalists preferred "the well-trained free black . . . subject to dismissal for misconduct," to "the slothful slave, who has no fear of loss of place."

about two thousand in 1850, most were far more skilled than free blacks in the rest of the Lower South. Some became quite wealthy as clothiers, grocers, and real estate speculators. They were able to purchase land and join the planter class, using slaves to work their vast acreage. One such planter, Antoine Dubuclet, was one of the wealthiest free blacks in the United States. His plantation was valued at $206,000 in 1860, a time when the estate of the average southern white man was valued at about $4,000. Dubuclet spent much of his time in his lavish New Orleans townhouse while the one hundred slaves he owned worked his sugar plantation.

The Creole culture in New Orleans produced a small, free black high society unlike any other in the United States. For the large majority who did not belong to the upper classes, though, life was an ongoing struggle for employment, education, equality, and dignity. Faced with competition from immigrants, prejudice from employers, and institutionalized racism, urban free people of color had limited opportunities to live on equal terms with white Americans.

Chapter Three

Out on the Western Frontier

Between 1800 and 1865, the area west of the Appalachian Mountains was populated by explorers, fur traders, early settlers, and gold miners. Among these western explorers were fugitive slaves, manumitted free people of color, and freeborn blacks. These African Americans were part of the larger American migration to the West. Like other western travelers, they moved for the promise of free land, the quest for adventure, and the dream of riches in the California goldfields. Many blacks were also motivated by the desire to escape slavery. Although life was often difficult, tedious, and lonely on the western frontier, free blacks were sometimes able to obtain a more dignified existence, unburdened by the prejudicial constraints placed on them in the East and South.

The U.S. census of 1850 shows a negligible population of free blacks living in the West: twenty-two people in New Mexico, forty-five in Nevada, fifty in Utah (mostly in Salt Lake City), and forty-eight in Colorado. California was home to the most free blacks, about one thousand, who flocked there following the discovery of gold in 1848. These low numbers may be inaccurate, however, because free blacks who were roaming explorers, trappers, fur traders, and miners were undoubtedly missed by census takers.

The Explorers

The first free people of color known to have traveled the American continent west of the Mississippi accompanied American explorer John C. Frémont on three expeditions. In 1838 and 1839 Frémont, known as the "Pathfinder," explored the regions between the Mississippi and Missouri rivers. From 1841 to 1846, Frémont led an expedition along the Oregon Trail into California's Sierra Nevada range.

Among those who accompanied Frémont through Wyoming, Idaho, Oregon, Nevada, and Utah were several free black men. One, Mifflin Gibbs, later became a well-known businessman and abolitionist newspaper publisher in California. Another member, Saunders Jackson, joined the exploratory party in order to raise $1,700 to purchase his wife and children from a slave owner in Missouri. Although the expedition did not pay Jackson that amount, he struck gold in California within days of traveling there. Taking his earnings, he immediately left for Missouri to

In 1846 John C. Frémont arrives with his expedition team in Monterey, California. The first free blacks to cross the Mississippi River were part of Frémont's expeditions.

buy his family's freedom. The Jackson family is believed to have later returned to California.

Perhaps the most celebrated black man to travel with Frémont was Jacob Dodson, one of the first well-known black cowboys. In 1842 Frémont described Dodson's abilities, saying he was "expert as a Mexican with a lasso, sure as a mountaineer with the rifle, equal to either on horse or foot, and always a lad of courage and fidelity."[29] Dodson performed such amazing feats as riding 840 miles, from Los Angeles to Monterey and back, in nine days.

The Fur Trappers

Fur trappers followed explorers in the great western migration of the nineteenth century. These men, though mostly illiterate, pos-

---

"A Perfect Woodsman"

In the 1820s, when the West was largely unexplored by Americans, Edward Rose worked as a fur trapper, military interpreter, and guide for several fur companies. As a free black, Rose lived for three years with the Aricaras Indians in present-day western South Dakota, where he spoke their language and practiced their customs. In 1845 Captain Reuben Holmes of the U.S. Army described Rose's character and abilities, reprinted here from *The Black West* by William Loren Katz.

> Rose possessed qualities, physical and mental, that soon gained him the respect of the Indians. He loved fighting for its own sake. He seemed in strife almost recklessly and desperately to seek death where it was most likely to be found. No Indian ever preceded him in the attack or pursuit of an enemy. He was as cunning as the prairie wolf. He was a perfect woodsman. He could endure any kind of fatigue and privation as well as the best trained Indians. He studied men. There was nothing that an Indian could do, that Rose did not make himself master of. He knew all that Indians knew. He was a great man in his situation.

---

sessed an intimate knowledge of the wilderness. They searched the woodlands for beaver, fox, otter, mink, bear, deer, cougar, and other animals whose pelts were in high demand by fashionable men and women in the East and in Europe.

Free black fur traders were exploring the wilderness as early as 1673 when five accompanied Louis Joliet, the first white man to journey down the Mississippi River. In later years free blacks worked in many different aspects of the fur trade, laboring as voyagers, independent hunters, traders, and interpreters. White fur traders often employed blacks to trade with Native Americans because the indigenous people were less suspicious and more receptive to blacks, who, like Native Americans, had a low status in American society. Writing in 1888 about the thirty years he had spent living among the trappers, Colonel James Stevenson said, "[The] old fur traders always got a Negro if possible to negotiate for them with the Indians, because of their 'pacifying effect.' They could manage [the Indians] better than the white man, with less friction."[30]

One such man was George Bonga, who resided in the north woods near present-day Leech Lake, Minnesota. Born in 1802, Bonga spoke English, French, Ojibwa, and several other Native American languages. He was married to a Minnesota Ojibwa woman. Bonga worked for the largest trading company of the day, American Fur Trading Company, maintaining trading posts at three lakes in the north woods. Six feet tall and weighing over two hundred pounds, Bonga was famous for his ability to carry ninety-pound packs of furs through the wilderness. But it was his intellect and diplomacy that proved useful to territorial governor Lewis Cass, who hired Bonga to interpret and negotiate treaties with several tribes who lived in the Lake Superior region.

At least one free black explorer did more than negotiate with Native Americans. James P. Beckwourth, a mulatto born in 1798, lived with the Crow in present-day Montana. Beckwourth was on a fur trapping expedition in about 1824 when he was captured by a party of Crow warriors. The trapper was mistakenly believed to be the long lost son of a tribal chief, Big Bowl. Writing about the incident in 1856, Beckwourth asked, "What could I do under the circumstances? . . . Even if I should deny my Crow origins, they would not believe me."[31]

Beckwourth spent the next six to eight years with the tribe, rising to the position of war chief as a reward for his bravery on the battlefield, having killed many Blackfoot enemies with his battleax. By his own account, he was later elevated to head chief of the tribe and married to ten women. Beckwourth finally left the Crow, accompanying Frémont for a time, and fighting for California's independence from Mexico in the 1840s. He is most remembered, however, for discovering a pass through the Sierra Nevada range, which bears his name. Beckwourth Pass was later used by thousands of gold seekers as they streamed into California during the gold rush.

The Rush to California

Free blacks and slaves played important roles in California from the earliest days of European settlement. Blacks were on the first Spanish expeditions to the state, and a census from 1790 stated that 18 percent of California's non-Indian population was of African ancestry. Among the forty-four people who founded Los Angeles in 1781, twenty-six were mulattos and free people of color. They shared a common language, culture, and religion with the whites and Native Americans in the party, all of whom were Spanish subjects and practiced Catholicism. An early mulatto settler, Juan Francisco Reyes, served as mayor from 1793 to 1795. Original owner of the San Fernando Valley, Reyes traded the land to the Franciscan monks in 1797 so that they could establish a mission there.

In the following years, California's free blacks settled the region side by side with Europeans. By the end of the eighteenth century, Santa Barbara was about 20 percent black, while San Francisco was about 15 percent. Though the percentages of free blacks may be significant, California was very sparsely populated until the January day in 1848 that gold was discovered on the south fork of the American River near present-day Sacramento. Before the year was over, California's population doubled from about ten thousand to twenty thousand as gold seekers began to move to the state.

The pace of immigration picked up considerably in December 1848 when President James K. Polk, in a speech before Congress, declared: "Recent discoveries render it probable [that California's

During the California gold rush many free blacks worked as cooks, barbers, and domestic servants.

gold] mines are more extensive and valuable than was anticipated. The accounts of the abundance of gold in that territory are of such an extraordinary character as would scarcely command belief."[32]

"What a Change Has California Wrought"

The president's announcement set off a stampede to California of gold seekers from all over the world. The state's population jumped to about 225,000 in the following three years. About two thousand of these people were African Americans, and about half of this number were slaves. In *California's Black Pioneers*, Kenneth Goode describes the situation:

> On the overland journeys to California the slaves worked as cooks, barbers, and domestic servants. Some arrived without any hope of obtaining their freedom but there were many others who believed, based upon oral agreements with their masters, that if they worked in the goldfields a

certain number of years and paid a certain sum of money to their masters during that time they would be set free. Some slaves did earn enough in the goldfields or elsewhere not only to purchase their freedom but also the freedom of their families. Reverend Darius Stokes, a black preacher, reported that during the early 1850s blacks in California had sent "home" about three quarters of a million dollars to purchase the freedom of members of their families.[33]

These people paid as much as $2,000 for family members. One woman was able to secure the purchase of all eight of her children for $9,000, earning the money to do so by working as a laundress.

Even though some free blacks were successful miners, in the California goldfields competition was fierce and desperation and violence all too common. In this Wild West atmosphere, African Americans were not generally welcomed by white miners. Often, free blacks discovered that there was more money to be made providing services to miners in boomtowns. For example, the business of feeding hungry miners was a lucrative one, since most miners spent all their time in streams and claims searching for gold. Leonard Kip, an observer of the social life during the gold rush days, wrote:

A Negro cook is one of the most independent men alive. Being a rather scarce article, he can act pretty much as he pleases . . . and he is allowed to enter into certain [intimate relations with whites], which would ensure him a cowhiding [whipping] in almost any other part of the globe.[34]

The gold rush had an unusual leveling effect on race relations. Successful black miners could be seen gambling alongside white miners, and even being served by whites. This was noted by the unnamed author of the city column for the *Daily Alta California* newspaper in San Francisco, who wrote:

What a change has California wrought in the organization and feelings of society. We were very much amused yesterday at seeing a gentleman of the colored persuasion, decked in a full suit of broadcloth, and sporting a gold watch and chain, standing on the square having his boots blacked by a good-looking white man.[35]

"The Black City Hall"

The gold rush boom also offered opportunities for black women. While most labored in obscurity as laundresses and cooks, one woman, Mary Ellen "Mammy" Pleasant, remained a controversial public figure for nearly two decades. Pleasant began life as a southern slave whose obvious intelligence inspired her owner to provide her with an education in Boston. Forced to flee the East because of her activities working for the Underground Railroad, Pleasant arrived in San Francisco on April 7, 1852. At that time, the city had about forty thousand people (six men to every woman), seven hundred saloons and casinos, and about one murder every day.

As a light-skinned mulatto, Pleasant was able to pass for a white woman. She set up a boardinghouse that catered to the wealthiest and most influential men in San Francisco. A very charming woman, Pleasant was able to convince these men to hire free blacks in the city. Because she was able to obtain so many favors for people, she was nicknamed "The Black City Hall."

Pleasant used her profits to hire lawyers to free slaves and fight discriminatory laws. She also became a skilled businesswoman who speculated on real estate and loaned money at 10 percent interest to destitute miners. One of her more infamous business-es involved cultivating beautiful young women whom she called "protegés." For a fee, Pleasant would arrange marriages between her protegés and the newly rich miners and bankers who frequented her boardinghouses.

Rumors spread that Pleasant was worth the incredible sum of $30 million, the equivalent of a billionaire by today's standards. While this was probably an exaggeration, Pleasant was also remembered for fighting back against discrimination. On her way home from church one Sunday evening in 1864, Pleasant and three other women decided to board a streetcar. They were quickly pushed off by the conductor, who told them that blacks were not allowed on the trolleys. Angered by the treatment,

A former slave, Mary Ellen Pleasant (left) ran a boardinghouse in San Francisco (right) that catered to the city's wealthiest and most influential men.

Pleasant returned with a lawyer and several witnesses and tried to board again. When she was evicted again, Pleasant sued and won monetary damages in a suit against the streetcar company. Although the company successfully appealed, because of Pleasant's initial actions, the California Supreme Court ruled in 1868 that blacks had equal rights to ride streetcars.

Building Community

The efforts of exceptional individuals like Pleasant sometimes made a remarkable difference in free blacks' prospects. However, churches and schools provided the most important community focus for California's free blacks. By the early 1850s, there were two African Methodist Episcopal (AME) churches and one Baptist church established in San Francisco, and one AME church in Sacramento. By 1860, free black Baptists had established churches in Stockton and Marysville, where AME churches had been also established. Although the congregations of these churches were small, the churches functioned as community centers for free blacks in California. As southern historian and author Rudolph M. Lapp notes:

A number of the ministers were well-educated and came to the West with experience in church work. They were tireless in their efforts to establish churches in areas throughout the state wherever Negroes were numerous enough to provide congregations.[36]

Spectacular Finds in the Goldfields

When California became a state in 1849, slavery there was outlawed. However, most of the constitutional convention was spent debating ways to prevent free blacks from either moving to the state or exercising civil rights once there. White miners were particularly vocal in asking legislators to ban blacks from the goldfields. Racial prejudice motivated the requests, but superstition and belief in luck also was a factor. It was believed that African Americans had some mystical ability to discover gold that gave them an advantage in the mining districts. Though the superstitions seem ridiculous, they were fueled by stories of several black men who made spectacular gold finds. In 1851, for example, one unnamed man allegedly had a dream in which he found a large pile of gold next to a cabin. When he had the same dream several nights later, he bought the cabin, demolished it, and began digging on the site. In less than a month the man found $80,000 worth of gold. Another story involved ten black sailors who abandoned their ship in order to strike it rich in the goldfields. Two of the miners, Charles Wilkins and Albert Callis, found huge quantities of gold that were simply sticking out of the earth. Both became extremely rich.

The spectacular stories of the few lucky black miners generated so much prejudice that many free blacks chose to stay away from the goldfields. Some of them discovered that it was easier to make money feeding, clothing, housing, and entertaining miners than by performing the backbreaking labor to search for gold. As such, some free blacks earned substantial incomes working as independent cooks, barbers, laundresses, and seamstresses.

The churches took a special interest in education since black children were generally barred from white schools. For example, although the first public schools were established in San Francisco in 1848, black children were not allowed to attend. It was not until 1854 that the first schools to teach African American students were opened by churches in San Francisco and Sacramento. Soon after, private schools were also opened in San Jose, Grass Valley, Oakland, and other cities where blacks had settled.

Oftentimes, once the schools were established, white-controlled boards of education took over the schools and made them part of the public school system. However, they continued to run them on a segregated basis; the separation of the races at school was rigorously maintained. In towns such as Watsonville, where there were few African Americans, white schoolteachers would visit black students in their homes in order to give lessons. Discrimination was also seen in school administration policies. While white teachers were paid $75 a month, black teachers were paid only $60.

Although there was hardly any integration in public schools, white administrators feared the prospect. In 1860 the state's superintendent of public instruction successfully petitioned the state legislature to pass a law that allowed him to withhold public funds from any school district that admitted blacks, Chinese, or Indians to white schools.

Excluded from white establishments, California's free blacks formed other organizations in order to enrich their lives. In 1849, when San Francisco was still a small town, thirty-seven black citizens formed a Mutual Benefit and Relief Society to aid newcomers and provide financial aid and assistance to those in need. Within the next five years, as the city's population climbed to 100,000, a cultural center was established that housed eight hundred books in its library. As with the black organizations in the East, those who belonged to the cultural center were expected to be of high moral character, and to improve their intellect by reading the organization's newspapers and books.

San Francisco was also home to three black newspapers, all carrying an antislavery and civil rights message. One of them, the *Mirror of the Times*, was established in 1855 by Mifflin W. Gibbs. Born in 1828, Gibbs traveled with John C. Frémont to California

A preacher in a church in Cincinnati delivers a rousing sermon to his congregation. The church served as a focal point in newly formed communities of free blacks.

in 1850 with little more than the clothes on his back. He made enough money shining shoes, however, to open a store that sold imported boots and shoes from London and New York. However, the political situation for African Americans in California continued to worsen during the 1850s, prompting Gibbs to start a newspaper to crusade for equal rights.

During this time, the state legislature approved one bill after another that discriminated against African Americans. The state constitution restricted voting rights to "free white males," thus excluding all nonwhites and women. The legislature also

The Remarkable Deeds
of Biddy Mason

In the nineteenth century, Biddy Mason's rags-to-riches story was well known to free blacks in the West. Mason was a slave who walked from Mississippi to California behind a massive, three-hundred-wagon train owned by her master. Once there she won freedom for herself and her three daughters by petitioning a sheriff with a writ of habeas corpus, a legal maneuver that releases a party from unlawful restraint. Leaving gold country, Mason moved to Los Angeles. Southern historian Rudolph M. Lapp continues the story in Bracey et al.'s *Free Blacks in America, 1800–1860*.

> Biddy Mason engaged in the occupation of nurse and mid-wife to the best families of the city. Noted for her works of charity, she frequently visited the jail where she spoke words of encouragement to the prisoners. So devoted was she to such deeds of mercy that she became widely known as "Grandmother Mason." In times of great distress for some unfortunates of the city, she would open an account at a store so that the poor could obtain supplies at her expense. But despite this unusual charity, she amassed considerable wealth. She bought a share in a large plot of land and later

adopted state testimony laws that prohibited blacks, mulattos, and Native Americans from testifying in any civil or criminal proceeding either for or against a white man. Free blacks were also barred from the state militia.

Gibbs used the *Mirror of the Times* to criticize these laws and to organize drives to petition the legislature for full civil rights. He also used his paper to help organize a statewide California Convention of Colored Citizens to protest government racism and discrimination. By 1858, however, the persecution of California blacks impelled Gibbs to move to Victoria on Vancouver Island in Canada. He quickly made a fortune in real estate and mining.

In the years after Gibbs's departure, California became the major center of free people of color in the West, although the secured the rest of it, along with other properties, which increased in value with the growth of the city. At the time of her death, she possessed property valued at $300,000. [Black historian] Delilah Beasley commented: "She is the most remarkable person of African descent, who came to the Pacific Coast before the Civil War, and was associated with many of the significant civic movements. It was in her home that the First Negro African Methodist Episcopal Church in the city of Los Angeles was organized."

Biddy Mason was a former slave who made a large fortune for herself in California real estate.

population was never over several thousand until after the Civil War. Like other Americans seeking their fortunes in the West, blacks were trappers, miners, and explorers. Unlike white settlers, people of color had to fight against not only the dangers posed by nature but also the prejudice and discrimination perpetuated by the majority. It took grit and determination to build schools, churches, and communities where the odds were stacked against their survival.

Chapter Four

Serving Their Country

Black soldiers, both free and slave, served in every conflict fought on American soil in the eighteenth and nineteenth centuries. Black men fought the French and their Native American allies in the French and Indian Wars of 1756–1763, and fought on both sides of the American Revolution. They served honorably as sailors and soldiers in the War of 1812, fought in the Southwest and California during the Mexican-American War, and saw combat on both sides of the Civil War. These black Americans were highly motivated soldiers, as Booker T. Washington states: "In most of these wars . . . the Negro has fought not merely in the interest of the country and of the civilization with which he has become identified, but also, as in the Revolutionary and Civil wars, to secure and maintain his own freedom."[37]

The history of American military service is marked by periods in which various laws excluded blacks from military service. In times of manpower shortage or great danger, however, laws were set aside and white leaders willingly called for black volunteers. At such times, black and white soldiers often served side by side, but there were also all-black units, many of which were honored for their bravery in battle. Free blacks were paid, though less than white soldiers, and slaves who served—and survived—were sometimes manumitted at the end of the war.

Crispus Attucks: "Foremost in Resisting"

The struggle that American colonists fought against their British rulers began in earnest on October 1, 1768, when British forces occupied Boston to quell the revolutionary stirrings of the citizens. Boston's civilians treated the soldiers as invaders, and for the next eighteen months there were often clashes between the two sides. On March 5, 1770, tensions reached a peak as a crowd of rowdy men demonstrated on Boston's town square, where British soldiers stood with loaded muskets. Leading the demonstration was forty-six-year-old Crispus Attucks, a former slave from Massachusetts who had been a freeman since 1750, working on a whaling ship that arrived in Boston in February 1770.

British soldiers fire on former slave Crispus Attucks and his band of protesters during the Boston Massacre of October 1768.

The whaler had attended several demonstrations against the British and at one protest, Attucks gave a brief speech about resisting the British and urged his fellow Americans to join together in resistance.

Attucks led a group of about sixty men to Boston's Custom House and began throwing chunks of ice, snowballs, and rocks at a group of soldiers who approached the scene. According to an eyewitness known only as Botta,

> [A] band of the populace, led by a mulatto named ATTUCKS, . . . brandished their clubs, and pelted [the British redcoats] with snowballs. The maledictions, the imprecations, the execrations of the multitude, were horrible. In the midst of a torrent of invective from every quarter, the military were challenged to fire. The populace advanced to the points of their bayonets. The soldiers appeared like statues . . . at length, the mulatto and twelve of his companions, pressing forward, environed the soldiers, and striking their muskets with their clubs, cried to the multitude: *"Be not afraid; they dare not fire: why do you hesitate, why do you not kill them, why not crush them at once?"* [Attucks] lifted his arm against Capt. Preston, and having turned one of the muskets, he seized the bayonet with his left hand, as if he intended to execute his threat. At this moment, confused cries were heard: *"The wretches dare not fire!"* Firing succeeds. ATTUCKS is slain. The other discharges follow. Three were killed, five severely wounded, and several others slightly. . . . ATTUCKS . . . had been foremost in resisting, and was first slain. As proof of a front engagement, he received two [musket] balls, one in each breast.[38]

Attucks today is recognized as "the first to defy, the first to die," in the American Revolution, according to a monument erected to him on Boston Commons in 1888. He was lauded as a true martyr, "the first to pour out his blood as a precious libation on the altar of a people's rights."[39] Despite prejudicial laws prohibiting the interment of blacks in Boston's Park Street cemetery, Attucks was buried there along with the other honored dead from what became known as the Boston Massacre.

The Rhode Island Battalion

In 1775 other freemen joined colonial forces and were present at every battle from Lexington and Bunker Hill to the final combat at Yorktown. At the beginning, however, General George Washington and other leaders were loath to let blacks join the Continental army. But the severe shortage of manpower motivated individual state legislatures to draft black men into militias. Many African Americans were eager to go to war for the promise of equal rights. As a free black Revolutionary War veteran known as Dr. Harris said in a speech in 1829:

A severe shortage of able-bodied men prompted state legislatures to draft black men into their militias.

Then liberty *meant* something. Then, liberty, independence, freedom, were in every man's mouth. They were the sounds at which they rallied, and under which they fought and bled. They were the words which encouraged and cheered them through their hunger, and nakedness, and fatigue, in cold and in heat. The word slavery then filled their hearts with horror. They fought because they would not be slaves. Those whom liberty has cost nothing, do not know how to prize it.[40]

With thousands like Harris ready to join the cause, Massachusetts began drafting free blacks in 1777, and in 1778 Rhode

Island passed a law allowing slaves to join the Continental army. Slaves who took up the offer were given salary and benefits equal to that of white soldiers, and in a precedent-setting move, they were instantly emancipated.

Records show that the ex-slaves who made up the Rhode Island First Regiment served honorably and with great distinction from 1778 until the end of the war in 1783. With five years of uninterrupted service, the Rhode Island First stayed together longer than most white units that served in the Continental army. It was present at many key battles, including Fort Oswego, New York, and

Lord Dunmore's Ethiopian Regiment

At the beginning of the American Revolution, the colonial army was reluctant to recruit black soldiers. However, Lord Dunmore, the royal governor of Virginia, had no such problem signing up blacks for the British cause. In November 1775 Dunmore issued a proclamation freeing all indentured servants and blacks in Virginia, inviting them to join the British army in order to force the colonists to obey the will of King George III. Dunmore's decree inspired thousands of slaves to run away, some with their owners' guns, ammunition, and clothing. In two Virginia counties alone, two thousand slaves ran away within weeks of the proclamation.

The slaves escaped to British ships, and about three hundred of these men formed a black fighting force known as Lord Dunmore's Ethiopian Regiment. Their uniforms proudly displayed the inscription "Liberty to Slaves" over their breasts. Though Dunmore had high hopes for the regiment, his plan was thwarted by a smallpox epidemic that swept through the black population, hitting hardest those who lived aboard overcrowded ships without warm clothing or sufficient food.

Despite this tragedy, slaves continued to run away, and by the end of the war, more than 100,000 enslaved people— nearly one in five—joined the British cause. Thomas Jefferson calculated that in Virginia in 1778 alone, more than thirty thousand blacks defected to the British side.

the final British defeat at Yorktown. At the Battle of Rhode Island, in which Continental troops were forced to retreat, a white soldier described the behavior of the soldiers in the First Regiment:

> *Three times in succession* they were attacked, with most desperate valor and fury, by well disciplined and veteran troops, and three times did they successfully repel the assault, and thus preserve our army from capture. They fought through the war. They were brave, hearty troops.[41]

"Valor and Good Conduct"

When the war finally ended, the black soldiers—like their white counterparts—were simply sent on their way with no compensation for their service. At the final address to the troops, white regiment commander Jeremiah Olney praised the soldiers' "unexampled fortitude and patience through all the dangers and toils in a long and severe war. . . . [He also declared] his [deep admiration] of their valor and good conduct displayed on every occasion when called to face an enemy in the field."[42]

Olney also expressed his profound regret that the troops would likely never receive the wages and back pay owed to them, and he promised to petition Congress to settle the accounts of the men in the regiment. Then, as Paul Finkelman and Lorenzo J. Greene write in *Slavery, Revolutionary America, and the New Nation,*

> Hungry, penniless, ragged, some of them sick or injured, [the black soldiers] began the hot, dusty march back to Rhode Island. There . . . [they] fought to restrain their erstwhile masters from reenslaving them. Gradually they lapsed into oblivion, forgotten by the ungrateful nation for which they had sacrificed so much to establish.[43]

While the fighting force of the Rhode Island First was unique, most free black soldiers suffered special hardships. They were never promoted beyond the rank of private, and often remained nameless, carried on the books as "A Negro Man," "Negro by Name," or "A Negro name not known."[44] Few were allowed to fight on horseback in the cavalry, but some served with artillery regiments, operating the big guns. Most often free people of color served in the infantry, barred from carrying guns but acting as waiters, cooks, or personal attendants to officers.

In the chaotic conditions of the American Revolution, social conventions were set aside and free blacks were able to gain an unprecedented degree of respect based on their military service. However, they were caught in a political tug-of-war between the Americans and the British, and both sides mistreated them. When the Revolution was over and white Americans were given their freedom from British rule, free blacks discovered that the poetic words in the Declaration of Independence were not written for them. Those who had helped fight the war returned to their lowly status as freemen trying to survive in a world of prejudice and discrimination.

"Absolutely Insensible to Danger"

In the years following the American Revolution, the federal government and many states passed laws prohibiting free blacks from serving in the army, Marine Corps, or state militias. They were not excluded from the navy, however, and once again free blacks were asked to serve their country when the United States was threatened.

In 1807 Great Britain began seizing American sailors from merchant ships at sea and impressing them, or forcing them into military service in the British navy. The seizures, and other issues, sparked the War of 1812, which was primarily a naval war fought on and around the Great Lakes, although the British did briefly invade Washington, D.C., and set fire to the White House, partially destroying it in 1814.

Like other American seamen, black sailors were targets of British impressment. This was particularly dangerous for black sailors, as Gerard T. Altoff writes in *Among My Best Men: African Americans and the War of 1812:*

> While black seamen might have managed to attain a semblance of equality, life was still characterized by toil, brutality, and deprivation. Black and white sailors alike took their chances if their ship was waylaid by an English man-o'-war on the high seas, but black seamen had more cause to worry and . . . faced an uncertain future, which might

During the Battle of Lake Erie in 1813, Oliver H. Perry and some of his crew row out to his ship, the *Niagara*. Black sailors comprised a large part of the ship's crew.

include [being sold into] slavery, imprisonment, or impressment.[45]

When the war began on June 18, 1812, many black seamen joined the U.S. Navy. The Americans needed every sailor they could find if they were going to battle with what was then the world's naval superpower: The British navy had 650 warships, while the U.S. Navy had 17. Despite the desperate need for manpower, a few influential ship captains rejected black recruits and kept their crews all white. Most did not, however, and as on commercial vessels of the time, about 15 to 20 percent of navy sailors were black.

The hardest fought and bloodiest battles of the war took place on Lake Erie as American forces attempted to annex Canada. Free black sailors were present in all battles fought on the Great Lakes, including the decisive victory of Master Commandant Oliver Hazard Perry on September 10, 1813. In a three-and-a-half-hour battle with 80 percent casualties near Put-in-Bay, Ohio, Perry's men managed to capture a six-ship British squadron that, until that time, controlled shipping on Lake Erie. The victory forced the British from the region and is credited as a turning point in the war. Perry spoke of the free black sailors who formed a large part of his crew: "They seemed absolutely insensible to danger. When [defeated British] Captain Barclay came on board [my ship] the *Niagara*, and beheld the . . . partly colored beings around him, an expression of chagrin escaped him at having been conquered by such men."[46]

"They Fought Like Desperadoes"

Free blacks were also among the land forces in the war, although black recruitment was against official army policy. About two thousand black soldiers fought in two regiments in New York, and hundreds participated in the famous last battle of the war in New Orleans. Fought on January 8, 1815, more than two weeks after the war had ended, the Battalion of Free Men of Color played a crucial role in the American victory.

The battalion had a long history, having been formed by the French in 1729 in order to fight the local Natchez and Chickasaw Indians. The battalion also fought, under Spanish command, against the British in the American Revolution. When Louisiana passed to the United States in 1803, the state legislature officially recognized the Battalion of Free Men of Color, the first time in American history that a black volunteer militia with black officers was authorized by a state.

During the War of 1812, New Orleans was continually threatened by British troops. Despite the danger, local residents refused to enlist the services of the Free Men of Color. However, American commander Andrew Jackson had strategic reasons to join forces with the black militia, writing: "They will not remain quiet spectators of the interesting contest. . . . They must be for, or against us. [The British will try to recruit them, and in the end] the country who extends to them equal rights and privileges with white men would win their loyalty."[47]

News of the British surrender had not reached either side when the British engaged American forces fighting with the Free Men of Color in the 1815 Battle of New Orleans. Despite being greatly outnumbered, the Americans prevailed and the British suffered a bloody, humiliating defeat. In its account of the battle, the Baltimore *Niles' Weekly Register* described the bravery of the free black soldiers who were casualties:

[The] killed and wounded on our part were chiefly of the New Orleans colored regiment who were so anxious for glory that they could not be prevented from advancing our breastworks [breast-high fortifications] and exposing themselves. They fought like desperadoes and deserved distinguished praise.[48]

Although the city was saved, when the British troops went home, they took two hundred slaves, kidnapped randomly from free blacks and slaves among the population. In the following years the contribution of the Battalion of Free Men of Color was quickly forgotten. Black veterans were even denied permission to participate in the annual parades held to celebrate the victory.

"Men of Color, to Arms!"

In the decades that followed, black soldiers continued to serve in the military, fighting Native Americans from Florida to California and defeating Mexico in the Mexican-American War. Meanwhile, the issue of slavery divided the United States into pro- and anti-slavery states. Six weeks after Abraham Lincoln was elected president in November 1860, six southern states seceded from the Union, setting off the Civil War. When Lincoln called for seventy-five thousand men to join the military to fight the war, he envisioned a short conflict and refused to consider black troops, stating, "This War Department has no intention at present to call into service of the Government any colored soldiers."[49] The president was afraid that border states that had not seceded would do so if black soldiers were put under arms to kill white Americans.

As in earlier conflicts, some states ignored federal policy and organized their own battalions. Early in January 1863, Massachusetts ordered the formation of the Fifty-Fourth Massachusetts Volunteer Infantry composed of "persons of African descent."[50] In addition to Massachusetts residents, volunteers came from many northern states. Some were acting in response to a March proclamation titled "Men of Color, to Arms!" issued by ex-slave and prominent abolitionist Frederick Douglass. The decree urged free blacks to join the fight, and among the recruits were two of Douglass's sons, Lewis H. and Charles R. Douglass.

Prompted by the success in Massachusetts, the federal government changed its policy. In May 1863 the War Department created

"Men of Color, to Arms!"

On March 21, 1863, renowned abolitionist Frederick Douglass issued a call for free blacks to join the Union army. It is reprinted on TeachingAmericanHistory.org.

Men of Color, To Arms!

A war undertaken and brazenly carried on for the perpetual enslavement of colored men, calls logically and loudly for colored men to help suppress it. . . . There is no time to delay. The tide is at its flood that leads on to fortune. From East to West, from North to South, the sky is written all over, "Now or never." Liberty won by white men would lose half its luster. . . . This is the sentiment of every brave colored man amongst us. There are weak and cowardly men in all nations. We have them amongst us. They tell you this is the "white man's war"; and you will be "no better off after than before the war"; that the getting of you into the army is to "sacrifice you on the first opportunity." Believe them not. . . . In good earnest then, and after the best deliberation, I now for the first time during this war feel at liberty to call and counsel you to arms. By every consideration which binds you to your enslaved fellow-countrymen, and the peace and welfare of your country; by every aspiration which you cherish for the freedom and equality of yourselves and your children; by all the ties of blood and identity which make us one with the brave black men now fighting our battles in Louisiana and in South Caroline, I urge you to fly to arms, and smite with death the power that would bury the government and your liberty in the same hopeless grave.

a Bureau of Colored Troops to handle recruitment and organization of black regiments. The regiments were known as United States Colored Troops (USCT), and they were commanded by white officers. By the end of 1863, of the 300,000 men in the Union army, more than one-third, over 100,000, were free blacks.

Although they were fighting for their country, prejudice persisted. Black privates were paid $10 per month, with $3 deducted for clothing. White privates were paid $13 per month and given an additional $3.50 for clothing. However, protests forced the army to grant black troops equal pay in 1864.

The first major engagement of the USCT was fought in May 1863, when eight regiments saw combat in Port Hudson, Louisiana. One of the regiments, the Louisiana Native Guard, took heavy losses that day, losing 129 men. One of the most desperate battles involving the Fifty-Fourth Massachusetts Regiment took place at Fort Wagner, South Carolina, on July 18, 1863. A description of the bloody battle was printed in the Boston newspaper *Transcript:*

[The] famous assault upon Fort Wagner, South Carolina, was made at twilight on the evening of July 18, 1863. In that assault Colonel Robert Gould Shaw fell dead upon the parapet. Captains Russell and Simpkins and other brave men fell while keeping the embrasures free from the enemy's gunners and sweeping the crest of the parapet with their fire. Lieutenant-colonel Edward H. Hallowell reached the parapet. Desperately wounded, he rolled into the ditch, was again hit, and with great difficulty managed to crawl to our lines. An unknown number of enlisted men were killed within the fort. Forty enlisted men, including twenty wounded, were captured within the fort. . . . The regiment went into action with twenty-two officers and six hundred and fifty enlisted men. Fourteen officers were killed or wounded. Two hundred and fifty-five enlisted men were killed or wounded. . . . The character of the wounds attests to the nature of the contest. There were wounds from bayonet thrusts, sword cuts, pike thrusts and hand grenades; and there were heads and arms broken and smashed by the butt-ends of muskets.[51]

"Fit for Freedom"

Despite the carnage, the number of free blacks participating in the Civil War continued to grow, as did the numbers of casualties. During the nearly two years that free blacks participated in all phases of the Civil War, thirty-seven thousand black soldiers died, almost 35 percent of all blacks who served in combat. Of the survivors, at

The Emancipation Proclamation

———————————■———————————

On January 1, 1863, in the midst of the Civil War, President Abraham Lincoln issued the Emancipation Proclamation, which stated that all slaves in the South were free. In reality, the Emancipation Proclamation did not free any slaves because the federal government did not control the southern Confederate states at that time. Most historians agree that the document was issued, in part, not only to express a moral purpose but also so that black slaves could enlist as soldiers in the Union army, which was experiencing a serious manpower shortage. This argument is supported by the third paragraph of the Emancipation Proclamation, which offered freed southern slaves not only moral support but practical incentive to join the Union cause:

> And I further declare and make known, that such persons of suitable condition, will be received into the armed service of the United States to garrison forts, positions, stations, and other places, and to man vessels of all sorts in said service.

least twenty-three received the Medal of Honor for their bravery in battle. Booker T. Washington was among those who believed that the bravery of the Civil War black soldiers helped convince the white majority that black people deserved equal rights:

> The services which the Negro troops performed in the Civil War in fighting for the freedom of their race not only convinced the officers who commanded them and the white soldiers who fought by their side that the Negro race deserved to be free, but it served to convince the great mass of the people in the North that the Negroes were fit for freedom. It did, perhaps, more than any other one thing to gain for them, as a result of the war, the passage of [the Thirteenth, Fourteenth, and Fifteenth] amendments to the Constitution which secured to the Negro race the same rights in the United States that are granted to white men.[52]

Chapter Five

Intellectuals, Inventors, and Innovators

From the earliest days of European settlement, the survival and prosperity of white America has depended on unique knowledge possessed by Africans, slaves, and free blacks. Even on the first European voyage to the Americas in 1492, a black man named Pedro Alonso Niño used his knowledge of astronomy, navigation, and sailing to pilot one of Christopher Columbus's three ships. In the 1600s, the success of the first white settlement in present-day Charleston was ensured by the complicated rice cultivation techniques perfected by black slaves from what was called the Rice Coast of West Africa. As Portia P. James writes in *The Real McCoy: African-American Inventors and Innovation, 1619–1930*: "By adapting African expertise to the new environment, African-Americans were able to contribute substantially to rice production. In fact, African-derived technology began to dominate rice cultivation in colonial South Carolina."[53]

In a land dependent on agriculture, many early inventions by blacks centered on crop planting, growing, harvesting, and processing techniques. Unfortunately, in a society based on slavery, the inventions of slaves were legally the property of their owners.

Slaveholders often took the credit—and the rewards—for the discoveries. For example, Anthony West, a slave owned by Benjamin Hunt in Charleston, made improvements to a grain threshing machine used in the 1830s. Hunt received the patent and earned large profits from his slave's innovations.

"Acquainted with Everything of Importance"

A few inventors were freemen who, through their unique status, were able to capitalize on their ingenuity. Benjamin Banneker, an astronomer, mathematician, and author, was probably the most famous free black intellectual in colonial America. Born in 1731 to a free mulatto mother and an African slave father who had purchased his freedom, Banneker grew up on a one-hundred-acre farm in the Baltimore region. His parents

Astronomer, mathematician, and author Benjamin Banneker was the most famous free black intellectual in colonial America.

ran a successful farming business raising tobacco, vegetables, fruit, and poultry.

Although education was denied to most free blacks in Maryland, Banneker attended an integrated, one-room school run by white Quakers. He attended only for a few months during the winter when his labor was not needed on the family farm. To make up for the shortened school year, Banneker spent most of his spare time reading rather than playing with other children. While performing monotonous tasks on the farm, he amused himself by making up difficult mathematical problems to solve.

When Banneker was still in his teens, he received an inspirational gift. In 1750 a traveling salesman gave the young man a pocket watch. This introduction to the latest technology fascinated Banneker. He took the watch apart and put it back together to better appreciate its intricate workings. In the two years that followed, Banneker built a large clock using the watch as a model. Each gear, movement, and chime was hand carved, and as Edward Sidney Jenkins writes in *To Fathom More:* "It should be kept in mind that most clocks and watches were made by skilled artisans. These technicians studied and practiced for years under the careful tutelage of master artisans . . . [and] had special tools and the right metals at their disposal."[54] Banneker had none of these and so carved the clock from wood, using exacting mathematical calculations to create a large-scale timepiece based on a small pocket watch. The finished clock was the only one of its kind in the United States, and people came from miles around to marvel at it. It kept perfect time for twenty years.

By the time he reached his early twenties, Banneker was more than a craftsman. He was a scholar familiar with mathematics and literary classics by William Shakespeare, John Milton, and others. Two men who worked at a local store, Charles Dorsey and George Ellicott, were always eager to talk with Banneker, as Dorsey noted:

He often came to the store to purchase articles for his own use, and after hearing him converse, I was always anxious to wait on him. After making his purchases, he usually went to the part of the store where George Ellicott was in the habit of sitting, to converse with him about the affairs of our government, and many other matters. He was very concise in conversation and exhibited deep reflection. His deportment, whenever I saw him, was perfectly upright and correct, and he seemed to be acquainted with everything of importance that was passing in this country.[55]

Many local farmers sought out Banneker to talk about matters more immediate than national politics. They asked his advice about technical affairs concerning farming, insects, weather, acreage, and building.

"The Man Who Saved Washington, D.C."

Banneker's father died in 1759 and Banneker spent most of his life running the family farm and supporting his mother. It was not until he was fifty-eight years old that Banneker was introduced to astronomy by George Ellicott, who lent him lunar tables, astronomical charts, and instruments such as telescopes. Studying late into the night after the farmwork was finished, Banneker quickly learned to plot the positions of the sun, moon, and planets and to predict solar and lunar eclipses. He also learned surveying, and when George Washington called together experts to build a capital city for the United States in present-day Washington, D.C., the free black mathematician was awarded a place on the commission. Using his knowledge of astronomy and surveying, Banneker plotted the locations of the Capitol building, the White House, the Treasury, and other buildings.

Banneker's responsibilities expanded overnight when the lead engineer on the project, Major Pierre L'Enfant of France, quit abruptly and took his plans with him. With the dream of a capital city in jeopardy, Washington expected the project to be delayed at least two years, if not longer. After listening to the pessimistic forecast, Banneker told the president that he had seen the plans and could replicate them quickly. Washington was doubtful since the plans were incredibly complex and detailed. Banneker had a photographic memory, however, and within a few days new plans were in the president's hands. In the years that followed, Banneker's feat earned him the nickname "the Man Who Saved Washington, D.C."[56]

Banneker is perhaps most remembered for his almanacs, which are still available today. When he was sixty years old he published his first *Almanac and Ephemeris*, which contained a precisely calculated table used in navigation that showed the position of heavenly bodies on any given day. The almanac also included abolitionist essays, poems, literature, and information about weather, tides, foreign currency exchange rates, religious festivals, and medicine.

Banneker used his almanac to broadcast his political opinions, proposing that the government set up a department of peace to provide free schools and teach lessons to prevent war. Banneker was also an ardent abolitionist whose almanac convinced Thomas

Banneker Debates Jefferson

Throughout early American history it was a common belief among whites that blacks were intellectually inferior. This was elucidated by Thomas Jefferson, who wrote in 1781, "In reason [black people] are much inferior, as I think one could scarcely be found capable of tracing and comprehending the investigations of [Greek mathematician] Euclid." Ten years later, mathematician and astronomer Benjamin Banneker would change Jefferson's opinion. Banneker sent a copy of his *Almanac and Ephemeris* to Jefferson, reminding him of the words he had written in the Declaration of Independence. Banneker's letter is reprinted in *Created Equal: The Lives and Ideas of Black American Innovators*, by James Michael Brodie.

How pitiable it is to reflect that, although you were so fully convinced of the benevolence of the Father of mankind that you should at the same time counteract His mercies in detaining by fraud and violence so numerous a part of my brethren under groaning captivity and cruel oppression. When the tyranny of the British crown was exerted to reduce you to servitude, your abhorrence was so excited that you publicly held forth this true and invaluable doctrine . . . "We hold these truths to be self-evident, that all men are created equal, and that they are endowed by their Creator with certain inalienable rights; that among these are life, liberty, and the pursuit of happiness. . . ." The Almanac is a production of my arduous study. I have long had unbounded desires to become acquainted with the secrets of nature, and I have had to gratify my curiosity herein through my own assiduous application to astronomical study. I need not recount to you the many difficulties and disadvantages I have had to encounter.

Jefferson that blacks could be the intellectual equals of whites. As James writes, "Banneker became one of the first African-Americans to use his individual accomplishments as a weapon against the bogeyman of racial inferiority."[57]

Banneker published his almanac from 1791 to 1802, when he was too old to continue the work. During those eleven years, at least twenty-nine editions of his almanacs appeared with localized information for Philadelphia; Baltimore; Wilmington, Delaware; Trenton, New Jersey; and Richmond and Petersburg, Virginia. Banneker died in 1806 and was buried on his farm next to the cabin where he spent his entire life.

Poems on Various Subjects

Banneker was not the only free black intellectual to challenge the notion of racial inferiority. In fact, most abolitionists felt that publicizing examples of black genius was the best way to refute the allegations made by proslavery factions. As a result, there was a movement to highlight the literary, artistic, and scholarly accomplishments among free black intellectuals and, in the words of James, "assert themselves on the national consciousness."[58]

The child prodigy Phillis Wheatley was held up as the perfect example of black merit. Kidnapped by slave traffickers in Senegal, Africa, at the age of eight, the young girl was purchased in Boston to work as a servant and attendant for Susannah Wheatley. However, Phillis was so exceptionally smart that she was soon accepted as a member of the family and raised with the Wheatleys' two children. Educated in a Quaker school, Phillis displayed significant talents in reading, writing, and learning Greek and Latin. She began writing poetry at a young age and at the age of ten became a Boston sensation after writing a poem about the death of the evangelical preacher George Whitefield. By the age of thirteen, Wheatley had written thirty-nine poems, enough for a book.

No Boston-area publisher would accept Wheatley's work. However, a London book company published her poems in a book titled *Poems on Various Subjects, Religious and Moral.* This first volume of poetry ever published by an African American reflected the religious and classical background of Wheatley's education.

The young woman's words attracted international recognition and touched a nerve in the colonies. When Wheatley went on an abolitionist tour of England, one unnamed man who heard her read her poetry pointed out the hypocrisy of American revolutionaries acting as slave owners, stating: "If there be an object

A former slave, poet Phyllis Wheatley gained international recognition for her work.

truly ridiculous in nature, it is an American patriot, signing resolutions of independency with one hand, and with the other brandishing a whip over his frightened slaves."[59] In the colonies, Wheatley's book was used as proof that all slaves should be emancipated and provided with schooling and job training.

James Forten: Inventor and Abolitionist

Books and almanacs published by free blacks helped the antislavery movement because thousands of copies could be made available to the public. Free black innovation did not stop with literary achievements, however; some inventors changed the very way that all Americans lived. With the money made from their inventions, most went on to help the needy and to financially support the abolitionist cause.

There is little doubt that Wheatley's poems provided inspiration to James Forten as a young man. Slightly younger than

Wheatley, Forten was born free in Philadelphia in 1766 and also attended a Quaker school. Forten's father worked for a local sailmaker and taught his son the trade. Forten's schooling ended at age fourteen, however, when his father died, leaving his family penniless. In order to support himself and his mother, Forten joined the crew of the *Royal Louis*, a Revolutionary War ship with an integrated crew.

After the war, Forten went to work as a sailmaker with Robert Bridges, who had once employed his father. When Bridges retired, he sold the business to Forten. At this time, around

Born free, James Forten invented a device that simplified the process of outfitting ships with sails.

1798, Forten invented a sail-handling device that provided an efficient way to outfit ships with sails. Forten was soon worth the substantial sum of $300,000. A fervent abolitionist, he refused to allow the invention to be used on slave ships.

Forten spent freely to further his beliefs. He paid for the publication of thousands of abolitionist pamphlets and purchased emancipation for dozens of slaves. He also donated money to fund abolitionist newspapers and offered his home as a stop on the Underground Railroad.

The Forten Women

The Forten household was a center for abolitionist activities, and Forten's wife, Charlotte Vandine Forten, and three daughters, Margaretta, Harriet, and Sarah, were also prominent in the antislavery movement. In December 1833

Charlotte and her daughters helped establish the Philadelphia Female Anti-Slavery Society, the country's first integrated organization of women abolitionists. The PBS network's Web site describes the contributions made by the family:

> Margaretta was one of 14 women who drafted the [Philadelphia Female Anti-Slavery] Society's constitution and was an officer throughout the organization's history. Sarah served on the organization's governing board for two years. Harriet frequently co-chaired the Society's antislavery fairs. The Fortens also represented the Society as delegates to state and national conventions.
>
> Margaretta . . . supported the women's rights movement. . . . Sarah Forten Purvis was a writer. Starting at age 17, she composed numerous poems and articles for the [abolitionist newspaper] *Liberator.* . . . At least one of her poems, "The Grave of the Slave," was set to music by black band leader Frank Johnson.[60]

"The Greatest Invention"

The Forten women continued to profit from James's invention after he died in 1842. However, Forten never patented the sail-handling device to stop others from producing it. Although free blacks faced a number of restrictions, they were allowed to file for patents after the U.S. Patent Act was approved by Congress in 1790. However, it is unclear if any did so, since the race of the inventor was not noted when patents were granted. Historians believe that the first black person to receive a patent was Thomas Jennings, a New York City tailor and dry-cleaner. In March 1821 Jennings received a patent for a dry cleaning process. Like Forten, Jennings was an abolitionist who used the financial gains from his patent to fight slavery and racial discrimination.

While Jennings's patent made the dry-cleaning process more efficient, it did not change the world, as Norbert Rillieux's patent did in the 1840s. Rillieux was born in New Orleans in 1806, the son of a wealthy white engineer and a black slave mother. Unlike many slave owners who sold their mulatto progeny to avoid creating conflict within their families, Rillieux's father raised his son as a freeman. Since blacks could not receive an education in New Orleans, Rillieux was sent to Paris for schooling.

Following in his father's footsteps, Rillieux also became an engineer. At age twenty-four he received considerable notice for his study of steam engines and their practical applications to industry. For the next thirteen years, Rillieux worked on a method to efficiently refine sugar using steam technology. After many failed experiments, in 1843 he obtained a patent for a method of evaporating the water from sugarcane juice called the multiple-effect evaporator. This process created the crystalline, white sugar common today. James Michael Brodie explains the importance of the invention in *Created Equal: The Lives and Ideas of Black American Innovators*:

> Prior to Rillieux's invention, sugar was an expensive luxury, used only on special occasions. The old process used to make sugar . . . was a slow, dangerous, and costly exercise, usually performed by slaves. They worked over open, boiling kettles, ladling sugarcane juice from one container to another. A large number of workers were scalded to death by the boiling substance, while many more received severe burns. . . . The end product of this dangerous process was a dark, thick syrupy substance, looking more like caramel than the granulated form known today. The syrupy sugar was poured into cones to dry and was bought and sold in this condition.[61]

Rillieux's patent had a profound effect on the sugar industry, which at the time was dominated by Brazil and Haiti, where slave labor was cheap and plentiful. With the new process, the United States came to dominate the world sugar market. Despite his contribution, Rillieux received little respect. His name was rarely mentioned in technical journals regarding his breakthrough invention. At home in New Orleans, like all other free blacks, he was treated as a second-class citizen with few rights.

The message of racial hatred was especially pointed when Rillieux devised a plan to free New Orleans from its rampant mosquito problem. At the time, mosquitoes bearing yellow fever infested the New Orleans sewer system. Their deadly bites created yellow fever epidemics that killed tens of thousands of people

The First African American Professor

———————————————◼———————————————

Charles L. Reason was a brilliant free black mathematician who seemingly put aside his own career advancement in order to promote public education for free blacks. Nathan Johnson provides a short biography of the mathematician on the History of Mathematics Web site.

Charles L. Reason was an exceptionally bright young man. In 1832, at the age of fourteen, Reason became a mathematics instructor, paid a salary of $25 a year. Around 1840, in response to charges that black teachers were inefficient and incompetent, which Reason took personally, he founded a school to train teachers.

In 1847, Reason cofounded an organization to be known as the Society for the Promotion of Education Among Colored Children, which would oversee black schools in New York City. Two years later, Reason made history by becoming the first African American to become a professor at a predominantly white college. He was hired as . . . [an] adjunct professor of mathematics at the integrated New York Central College in McGrawville, New York. Reason's career there was relatively short-lived, however; three years later, he resigned and became the first principal of Philadelphia's Institute for Colored Youth (now known as Cheyney State University). . . . [He is credited with expanding enrollment from 6 to 118 students, improving the school's library, and attracting distinguished visiting speakers.] Reason finally found some stability when he returned to New York in 1855, serving thirty-seven years as a teacher and administrator in city schools.

over the years. Rillieux engineered a plan to improve the sewers and drain swamps around the city in order to dry up the breeding grounds for the mosquitoes. Inexplicably, state and city officials refused to award such a prominent contract to a free person of color. New Orleans residents continued to be plagued with yel-

African Cure for Smallpox

Smallpox killed tens of thousands of Native Americans and colonists in the eighteenth century. A Massachusetts slave named Onesimus learned an African method to prevent the disease from spreading. White Americans, however, refused to use the inoculation because it was proposed by a black man, as Portia P. James explains in *The Real McCoy*.

> [The] smallpox epidemic of 1721 was one of the worst ever to strike Boston. . . . That year, in the midst of the epidemic, the Puritan leader Cotton Mather tried to convince the city that inoculation—a practice first revealed to Mather by his slave, Onesimus—was an effective deterrent to the disease. Inoculation was a revolutionary concept in eighteenth-century New England, but . . . Onesimus's apparent immunity to smallpox . . . encouraged Mather to promote the practice among influential New England citizens.
>
> Mather wrote to a friend explaining how he came to know about the procedure:
>
>> *Enquiring of my Negro-man Onesimus . . . whether he ever had ye Small-pox he answered, both, Yes, and No; and then told me, that he had undergone an Operation, which had given him something of ye Small-Pox, & would forever Prae-serve him from it. . . .*
>
> Onesimus had originally explained the procedure to Mather in 1706: "People take the Juice of the Small-Pox; and Cut the Skin, and put in a drop . . . and no body dye of it; no body have small pox any more."
>
> Mather and others tried to alert medical practitioners to the life-saving opportunity that inoculation provided, but they were ridiculed for following the "superstitions" of Africans. Mather's advocacy of inoculation provoked a great deal of controversy and hostility in Boston; at one point, several proponents of the practice, including Mather, were threatened by mob violence.

low fever epidemics for many more years until a white person introduced virtually the same plan.

Disgusted by his treatment in the United States, Rillieux moved to France at the outbreak of the Civil War. Although he received little respect in the land of his birth, Rillieux's invention mechanized the sugar industry and freed thousands of slaves from sweltering, dangerous labor. Still used today to make sugar, soap, gelatin, condensed milk, and glue, it is no wonder that Charles A. Browne, a U.S. Department of Agriculture chemist, called the Rillieux evaporator "the greatest invention in the history of American chemical engineering."[62]

To Aid Inventors

Black inventors and innovators were as important to the abolition movement as intellectuals and writers, prompting abolitionist newspapers to print articles about black achievers. The leading abolitionist paper of the times, the *Liberator*, went further, running ads that requested information about "colored inventors of any art, machine, manufacture, or composition of matter . . . [in order to] collect proof of colored talent and ingenuity and . . . to aid colored inventors in obtaining their patents for valuable inventions."[63]

To proclaim the accomplishments of black innovators, groups also organized fairs such as the Colored American Institute for the Promotion of the Mechanical Arts and Sciences. Held in Philadelphia in April 1851, exhibits at the fair demonstrated the talents of black artisans, mechanics, and inventors. As James writes, free blacks "lauded such fairs as glimpses into the future achievements of a race freed from the constraints of slavery."[64]

Chapter Six

Fighting Slavery in Word and Deed

$\mathbf{T}$he economic success of the American colonies was primarily founded on slave labor. No matter how essential their work was to the country, however, there were always those who opposed slavery on moral grounds. The first organized group to speak out against the involuntary servitude of Africans were deeply religious women and men of the Quaker denomination. Formally called the Society of Friends, Quakers believed that slavery was sinful and evil. In 1688 Quakers from Germantown, Pennsylvania, drafted an antislavery petition that stated in part:

> To bring men hither [to America], or to rob and sell them against their will, we stand against. . . . Pray, what thing in the world can be done worse towards us, than if men should rob or steal us away, and sell us for slaves to strange countries; separating husbands from their wives and children.[65]

The Quakers remained the most persistent white critics of slavery well into the eighteenth century, their voices growing louder as the population of slaves continued to grow. Their dedication to the cause was so great that they risked arrest to help fugitive slaves escape bondage. Such activities attracted the attention of George Washington, who addressed this in 1786. Speaking of an escaped slave, Washington said, "a society of Quakers formed for such purposes, have attempted to liberate him."[66] Such actions prompted Congress to pass the Fugitive Slave Act in 1793. This law made it a crime to help an escaped slave or prevent his or her arrest. Those who broke the law were subject to heavy fines and imprisonment. Free blacks who broke the law could be arrested and sold into slavery themselves. Despite the law, however, the numbers of people, both black and white, who helped slaves escape bondage continued to grow.

During the 1830s, the abolitionist movement grew into a militant crusade. Substantial support for so-called antislave societies came from individual African Americans, churches, fraternal

In this eighteenth-century illustration, a group of Quakers gathers at an abolition meeting. The Quakers were the most persistent white critics of slavery.

societies, and benevolent organizations. Antislavery literature abounded, as did petitions demanding that Congress ban slavery. In response to the latter, the U.S. House of Representatives passed a "gag rule" that banned consideration of antislavery petitions. Abolitionist activities also provoked widespread hostility in both the North and South. Violent mobs broke up meetings and burned mailbags containing abolitionist literature.

Free Blacks and White Abolitionists

In addition to violence and official disregard, free blacks faced other obstacles. Many white abolitionists were paradoxically unwilling or afraid to interact socially with free black people. To openly participate in what was called race mixing might incite harsh scorn and violence that was said to harm the abolitionist cause. As Charles Follen admitted in a speech before the Massachusetts Anti-Slavery Society in 1836, abolitionists had been advised not to "shock the feelings, though they were but prejudices, of the white people, by admitting colored persons to our Anti-Slavery meetings and societies. We've been told that many who would otherwise act in union with us, were kept away by our disregard of the feelings of the community in this respect." Follen went on to condemn these attitudes, however, saying, "How can we have the effrontery to expect the White slave holders of the South to live on terms of civil equality with his colored slave, if we, the white abolitionists of the North, will not admit colored freemen as members of our Anti-Slavery societies?"[67]

Free black leaders, while appreciative of the work of the abolitionists, were not afraid to speak out against the prejudicial attitudes within the antislavery movement. As an unnamed free black teacher stated: "Even our professed friends have not yet rid themselves of [prejudice]. . . . To some of them it clings like a dark mantle obscuring their many virtues and choking up the avenues to higher and nobler sentiments."[68] Other free blacks complained that while abolitionists protested slavery in the South, they seemed blind to the segregation, discrimination, racism, and poverty forced upon northern blacks. As the newspaper *Colored American* charged in 1839:

At this moment more is known among abolitionists of slavery in the Carolinas, than of the deep and damning thrall-

The Petition for Freedom

While abolitionists worked to end slavery, slaves in the North sought their emancipation through legal means. On May 25, 1774, a group of black slaves sent a petition to the Massachusetts legislature asking for their freedom, which was not granted. The petition was reprinted with its original eighteenth-century style of spelling intact by Ray Raphael in *A People's History of the American Revolution*.

Humbly Shewing

That your Petitioners apprehend we have in common with all other men a naturel right to our freedoms without Being depriv'd of them by our fellow men as we are a freeborn Pepel and have never forfeited this Blessing by [any] compact or agreement whatever. But we were unjustly dragged by the cruel hand of power from our dearest [friends] and sum of us stolen from the bosoms of our tender Parents and from a Populous Pleasant and plentiful country and Brought hither to be made slaves for Life in a Christian land.

Thus we are deprived of every thing that hath a tendency to make life even tolerable, the endearing ties of husband and wife we are strangers to for we are no longer man and wife than our masters or mistresses thinkes proper marred or [unmarried]. Our children are also taken from us by force and sent [many] miles from us wear we seldom or ever see them again there to be made slave of for Life which sumtimes is [very] short by Reson of Being dragged from their mothers [breast]. Thus our Lives are imbittered to us on these accounts. . . .

We therfor [beg] your Excellency and Honours will give this its deer weight and consideration.

dom [subjugation] which grinds to the dust the colored inhabitants of New York. And more efforts are made by them to rend the physical chains of Southern slaves, than to burst the soul-crushing bondage of the Northern states.[69]

These harsh realities inspired many blacks to establish their own means to abolish southern slavery and to end northern oppression. Using newspapers, pamphlets, legislative petitions, conventions, and public speeches, free black activists made their voices heard.

The Convention Movement

National conventions were among the first coordinated efforts of black activists to assert their rights. During these large gatherings, orators spoke as free Americans, decrying slavery and racism while invoking the spirit of the American Revolution, the Declaration of Independence, and the Bill of Rights. According to one mission statement released by the 1853 Negro People's Convention in New York:

> We are Americans, and as Americans, we would speak to Americans. We address you not as aliens, or as exiles, humbly asking to be permitted to dwell among you in peace; but we address you as American citizens asserting their rights on their own native soil. Neither do we address you as enemies (although the recipients of innumerable wrongs), but in the spirit of patriotic goodwill.[70]

The convention movement began in 1817 as a reaction to the American Colonization Society, an organization formed by proslavery forces with the stated mission of sending free blacks back to Africa, where they could no longer agitate against slavery. Members of the Colonization Society included some of the most prominent men in America, including Andrew Jackson, James Monroe, and James Madison. In *Clarion Call*, Bella Gross explains the attitudes of the American Colonization Society, which claimed it was formed to aid "the free Negroes, who . . . had no place in our civilization, no protection from the cruelties inflicted upon them by white people who looked upon the free Negroes as their enemies, as outcasts, pariahs, aliens in an alien land. Their place [is] in Africa, their homeland. . . . [Why] not send them back to Africa?"[71]

Free blacks, most of whom were born and raised in the United States, were frightened and appalled by this concept. Many had fought for their country as soldiers, and few were willing to

A crowd of abolitionists listens as a speaker exposes the evils of slavery. A family of free blacks can be seen in the lower right of this illustration.

move. Africa was a poverty-stricken land where free blacks had no means of survival and knew neither the language nor the customs. Reacting to the Colonization Society, a convention by the American Society of Free Persons of Color was held in Philadelphia on August 10, 1817. During this first convention of its kind, speaker after speaker denounced the back-to-Africa movement and professed solidarity with their mothers, fathers, sisters, brothers, and other relatives who were still held in bondage. They also reasserted their American roots. As Samuel E. Cornish later wrote in the black abolitionist newspaper *Freedom's Journal*: "WE ARE AMERICANS . . . Many would rob us of the endeared name 'Americans,' a description more emphatically belonging to us, than to five-sixths of [the people now living in] this Nation, and one that we will never yield."[72]

The Philadelphia convention attracted national attention. It also inspired similar conferences in cities throughout the North and Upper South; antislavery meetings and protest demonstrations were held in Boston, New York, Albany, Baltimore, Hartford, and elsewhere.

In the following years, the American Society of Free Persons of Color played an active role in black abolitionism. The group held annual meetings and published its own constitution and guides for activists. Hundreds of auxiliaries with thousands of members were created in towns and cities throughout the nation. These groups worked at local and national levels. Members campaigned

A Call to the California Convention

Although there were only a few thousand free black people in California in the decades before the Civil War, many were participants in the convention movement popularized in the East. The following announcement by the Colored Citizens of California was a call to the state convention in 1855. It is reprinted in *California's Black Pioneers* by Kenneth G. Goode.

Brethren: Your state and condition in California is one of social and political degradation; one that is unbecoming a free and enlightened people. Since you left your homes and peaceful friends in the Atlantic States . . . you have met with one continued series of outrages, injustices, and unmitigated wrongs unparalleled in the history of nations. You are denied the right to become owners of the soil, that common inheritance which rewards our industry, the mainspring of all human actions, which is to mankind in this world like the action of the sun to the other heavenly bodies. You are compelled to labor and toil without any security that you shall obtain your just earnings as an inheritance for yourself or your children in the land of your birth.

Then, in view of these wrongs which are so unjustly imposed upon us . . . we call upon you to lay aside your various avocations and assemble yourselves together on Tuesday, the 20th day of November, A.D. 1855, in the city of Sacramento, at 10 A.M. for the purpose of devising the most judicious and effectual ways and means to obtain our inalienable rights and privileges in California.

to educate and train young people while fighting to obtain jobs for black laborers. On the national level, mass demonstrations such as the Negro Day of Prayer and Fasting were held in large cities. At these demonstrations, widely covered in the press, speakers castigated the colonization movement, demanded that slavery end, and called for jobs, education, and equality for all black people.

The conventioneers were able to point to some successes with their agenda. For example, the June 1831 Second National Negro Convention in Philadelphia raised $10,000 from white abolitionist groups, half the money needed to fund the Negro Manual Labor College, to be built in New Haven, Connecticut. (The school was never built because of violent opposition from racists, including New Haven's mayor.)

"Denounced as Traitors"

Whatever satisfaction conventioneers took away from the 1831 convention was soon eclipsed when forty Virginia slaves led by Nat Turner fomented a rebellion, stabbing, shooting, and clubbing at least fifty-five white people to death. The northern press, which had generally supported the free black organizations, suddenly turned vicious. According to Gross, the "conventions were denounced as the instruments and inciters of insurrection and ruin. . . . All white people who dared to raise a voice on their behalf were denounced as traitors and agents of massacre and rebellion."[73] This served as ammunition for the procolonization movement, which declared that the sooner the free blacks were sent back to Africa, the sooner peace would prevail in the slave states.

Such battles were indicative of the convention movement. Every year until the beginning of the Civil War, free blacks would hold conventions around the country. In the weeks that followed, according to historian Bella Gross, the backlash increased:

The pro-slavery-interests whipped up more and more excitement and hysteria, and increased the physical violence and terrorization to break the resistance of the free Negroes and their friends. More black laws were passed [restricting civil rights] . . . more federal support obtained for the colonizationists. So terrible were the results in some of the states that more astute politicians called a halt to the bloody persecutions, and demanded open, compulsory emigration laws to force all free Negroes out of the country, and strict laws against further emancipation.[74]

Frederick Douglass

Frederick Douglass was one of the most popular orators at black conventions. Born a slave in Maryland in 1817, he became one of the most famous African American abolitionists as well as one of the greatest American public speakers of his time. Douglass was taught the alphabet at a young age by his master's wife and later taught himself to read and write. In 1838 Douglass escaped to New Bedford, Massachusetts, where he came into contact with the Massachusetts Anti-Slavery Society. By 1841, the society enlisted Douglass as a public speaker because of his skillful oratory.

In speech after speech, Douglass told of the horrors of slavery and called for its immediate abolition. Rather than offering harsh words, however, Douglass offered poetic eloquence unmatched among most speakers of the day. An example can be found in Douglass's 1845 autobiography, *My Bondage and My Freedom*:

> The slave is bound to mankind by the powerful and inextricable net-work of human brotherhood. His voice is the voice of a man, and his cry is the cry of a man in distress, and man must cease to be man before he can become insensible to that cry. It is the righteousness of the cause—the humanity of the cause—which constitutes its potency. As one genuine bankbill is worth more than a thousand counterfeits, so is one man, with right on his side, worth more than a thousand in the wrong.[75]

Douglass's graceful fluency worked against him in some white abolitionist circles where audiences wanted to hear the stereotypical uneducated slave speak in the broken slang of the day. As one abolitionist told Douglass, "People won't believe you were ever a slave, Frederick. . . . Better to have a little of that plantation speech than not; it is not best that you seem too learned."[76]

To dispel this notion, Douglass published his autobiography containing vivid details of his life as a slave, including whippings, beatings, and his dramatic escape to freedom.

Douglass's book brought him international fame. He later traveled to the British Isles, where he became something of a celebrity for his antislavery speeches. Upon returning to the United States, he settled in Rochester, New York, and founded a newspaper, the *North Star* (later renamed *Frederick Douglass' Paper*). A true reformer to the end, Douglass collapsed and died on February 20, 1895, after attending a meeting organized to obtain voting rights for women.

An escaped slave, Frederick Douglass was one of the Massachusetts Anti-Slavery Society's most inspirational speakers.

The Underground Railroad

While living in Rochester, Frederick Douglass often offered his home as an Underground Railroad station. Like thousands of other free blacks, he risked his life to help fugitive slaves escape to the North.

What is known today as the Underground Railroad came into existence in the early 1830s. It was neither underground nor an actual railroad; legend has it that the railroad got its name when a slave named Tice Davis escaped from the slave state of Kentucky to the free state of Ohio. Davis's owner, whose name is unknown, concluded that Davis had escaped on an "underground road." The first steam-powered locomotive, the Tom

Thumb, had made a successful run in 1830 and before long the story was that Davis had escaped on an underground railroad.

There never was anything as comfortable or efficient as a railroad carrying slaves to freedom, but the term caught on. The journey had to be taken in strict secrecy, or "underground," and soon other railroad terms were applied to the journey. These terms were easy for slaves to remember and served to disguise the illegal activities of the railroad. Slaves were referred to as "parcels" or "passengers," while those who hid them and helped them were called "conductors." Homes that offered refuge were "depots" or "stations," and the people who lived there were "stationmasters."

Those who took advantage of the Underground Railroad often planned their escapes in great secrecy for years. Even planning carried considerable risk, as detection could mean beating, whipping, branding, or other cruel punishments. Slaves who put a plan into action and were lucky enough to make it to a depot maintained by a free black stationmaster were usually hidden in attics, barns, basements, and even secret rooms. After the fugitives were fed, clothed, treated for medical complaints, and

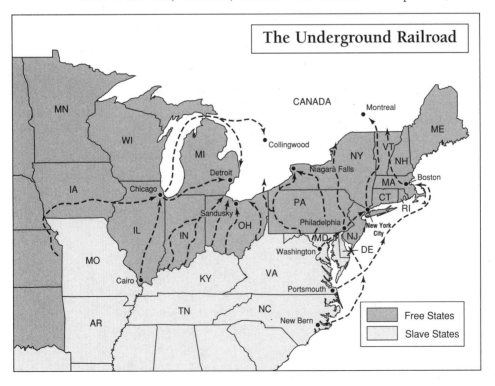

The Underground Railroad

Working as part of the Underground Railroad, a white family welcomes a group of fugitive slaves to the safety of their farm.

sometimes disguised, conductors would then accompany them to another station.

Passengers might be transported in wagons fitted with false bottoms or secret compartments that were covered with hay or other cargo. Most escapes involved several means of transportation, including horseback, covered wagons, large and small boats, carriages, and even trains, on which fugitives hid in boxcars or posed as free blacks using train tickets supplied by conductors on the Underground Railroad. To disguise their past, fugitives sometimes obtained forged papers that showed them to be free black persons, but this ruse was easily detected under the intense scrutiny of the slave hunters and was used only as a last resort.

Thousands of Underground Railroad depots dotted the American landscape. Many were African American churches where free blacks organized to help their brethren in bondage. At the Mt. Zion United AME Church, which still stands in Washington, D.C., fugitive slaves were hidden in the burial vault in the church's cemetery. In New York City, the Mother Zion AME Church holds the distinction of having sheltered hundreds of runaways after it was built in 1800. The Mother Bethel AME Church in Philadelphia, built in 1805, was also a major station on the Underground Railroad; large sums of money were raised to comfort the fugitives who were sheltered there.

Conductor Harriet Tubman

Former slaves often were the most enthusiastic conductors on the Underground Railroad. Harriet Tubman, known as the "Moses of Her People," was an escaped slave herself and one of the most famous free blacks in the United States. Tubman was born around 1821 in Dorchester County, Maryland, and escaped from slavery in 1849. She made her way ninety miles on foot to Philadelphia, where she worked by day as a cook in a hotel. At night, Tubman attended meetings of the Philadelphia Vigilance Committee, an abolitionist group.

Tubman occasionally heard news about her parents and brothers and sisters who were still living in bondage in Maryland. When she heard that her sister Mary and her children were about to be sold, possibly to a plantation farther south, Tubman volunteered to go rescue them. Refusing warnings from other committee members that it was too dangerous of a mission for an ex-slave, Tubman traveled to Baltimore to guide her sister and her family from station to station until they reached Philadelphia. The success of the mission gave her the courage to rescue other family members.

In autumn 1851, dressed like a man in a suit and hat, Tubman made her way back to the plantation she had first run away from. She found her brother John and his wife, but they were too afraid to leave. So instead, Tubman moved quietly through the plantation slave quarters knocking on doors. Soon she had collected a small group of slaves who desired their freedom and successfully navigated the long trek to Philadelphia.

Tubman returned south in December 1851 on another rescue mission. By this time, word had spread of her bravery and she was quickly becoming a legend among the slaves. Again, Tubman conducted a group north, traveling by night and hiding by day. They scaled mountains, forded rivers, and threaded their way through dense woodlands, hiding whenever pursuers passed them.

On this rescue mission, Tubman conducted eleven slaves to freedom, including another brother and his wife. Because a new influx of slave hunters was quickly making Philadelphia unsafe for fugitive slaves, Tubman took this large group all the way to St. Catharines in Ontario, Canada. Since it was late December and snow was falling, Tubman decided she could not abandon the ex-slaves. She and the others got jobs to pay rent on a small house and to put food on the table. Tubman was amazed by Canada, where black men could vote, hold office, sit on juries, and live wherever they chose. She decided to move to St. Catharines, and she based her operations out of that city for many years.

From 1852 to 1857, the woman called Moses returned twice a year to Maryland to bring back slaves—once in the spring and once in the

Throughout the 1850s, former slave Harriet Tubman helped more than three hundred slaves escape to freedom.

fall. Between trips Tubman worked in hotels to raise money for the journeys. Almost everyone she helped was a stranger to her. Tubman had an uncanny ability to sense when danger was near, and she was able to persuade hundreds of frightened fugitives to endure heat, cold, hunger, and fatigue in order to find freedom. Slaveholders eventually offered a $40,000 reward for Tubman's capture. This added a new element of danger to her operations.

By 1858 Tubman had conducted more than three hundred slaves to freedom, including her aged parents. Tubman's operation was so successful that the entire slave population of some Maryland regions escaped, causing a general panic among slaveholders. In December 1860 Tubman led her final group of runaways to freedom. The Civil War soon broke out, and Tubman served as a spy and a guide for the Union army in Maryland and Virginia. After the war, she managed a home for elderly blacks in Auburn, New York, until her death at the age of ninety-two in 1913. Tubman was buried with full military honors.

While many free blacks simply struggled to survive, Harriet Tubman, Frederick Douglass, and thousands of others fought slavery in word and deed. Without them, it is possible that the horrible details of slavery would never have been known to the majority of white Americans, especially those living in the North. With speeches, conventions, demonstrations, newspapers, and

Harriet Tubman (far left) helped this slave family escape to freedom. After the Civil War, Tubman founded a home to help care for elderly and poor blacks.

Freedom Journals

———■———

The free blacks who were the leaders of the abolitionist movement were often successful business leaders, scholars, and inventors. In addition to sponsoring national conventions, some were also editors and publishers of black newspapers and magazines. These publications acted as a forum to uplift the spirits of downtrodden people and to organize and petition against racism, slavery, and other ills.

The first black newspaper, *Freedom's Journal*, was published in 1827 by two black leaders, John Russwurm and Samuel E. Cornish. Russwurm was one of America's first black college graduates, and Cornish was an ordained minister in New York City's first African American Presbyterian church. During the two years that the paper was published, articles addressed issues important to the black community such as abolitionism, education, temperance, moral lessons, and historical and literary lessons. Newspapers run by free blacks had titles such as the *Rights of All*, the *Weekly Advocate*, the *Colored American*, the *Mirror of Liberty*, the *Alienated American*, and the *Weekly Anglo-African*. They were published in New York City, Philadelphia, Pittsburgh, Cleveland, Albany, San Francisco, and elsewhere. Typically the papers lasted for only a year or two before shutting down. Newspapers were difficult to keep afloat financially, and editors had to fight racism, mob violence, and vicious attacks in the white press. Despite the odds against them, black editors and publishers managed to provide news, information, editorials, and a sense of community to an often degraded and dispirited group of readers.

hazardous duty on the Underground Railroad, these patriotic Americans took the words of the Declaration of Independence and the Bill of Rights to heart. And by shedding light on those words, they forced the United States to end slavery on the American continent for all time.

Notes

Introduction:
Free People of Color

1. Quoted in Ira Berlin, *Slaves Without Masters*. New York: Pantheon, 1974, p. 5.
2. Booker T. Washington, *The Story of the Negro, Volume 1*. London: T. Fisher Unwin, 1909, p. 193.
3. Berlin, *Slaves Without Masters*, p. xiii.
4. Washington, *The Story of the Negro*, p. 200.

Chapter 1:
Free Blacks in the Countryside

5. Quoted in Writers Program of the Work Projects Administration in the State of Virginia, *The Negro in Virginia*. New York: Hastings House, 1940, p. 115.
6. Quoted in Writers Program, *The Negro in Virginia*, p. 116.
7. Emma Lou Thornbrough, *The Negro in Indiana*. Indianapolis: Indiana Historical Bureau, 1957, p. 135.
8. Quoted in Thornbrough, *The Negro in Indiana*, p. 136.
9. Berlin, *Slaves Without Masters*, p. 51.
10. Quoted in Berlin, *Slaves Without Masters*, p. 51.
11. Quoted in Berlin, *Slaves Without Masters*, p. 192.
12. Quoted in Berlin, *Slaves Without Masters*, p. 192.

13. Quoted in Paul Finkelman, ed., *Free Blacks in a Slave Society*. New York: Garland, 1989, p. 395.
14. Quoted in Horry County Historical Society, "Timber and Turpentine Industries," April 23, 1999. www.hchs online.org/places/turpentine.html.
15. Quoted in Horry County Historical Society, "Timber and Turpentine Industries."

Chapter 2: Working in the City

16. Berlin, *Slaves Without Masters*, p. 168.
17. Quoted in Finkelman, *Free Blacks in a Slave Society*, p. 5.
18. John M. Duncan, *Travels Through Part of the United States and Canada in 1818 and 1819, Volume 1*. London: Hurst, Robinson, 1823, p. 60.
19. Quoted in Finkelman, *Free Blacks in a Slave Society*, p. 5.
20. John H. Bracey Jr., August Meier, and Elliot Rudwick, eds., *Free Blacks in America, 1800–1860*. Belmont, CA: Wadsworth, 1971, p. 2.
21. Quoted in James Oliver Horton and Lois E. Horton, *Black Bostonians*. New York: Holmes & Meier, 1979, p. 28.
22. Horton and Horton, *Black Bostonians*, p. 34.
23. Christopher Phillips, *Freedom's Port*. Urbana: University of Illinois Press, 1997, p. 77.

24. Quoted in Phillips, *Freedom's Port*, p. 77.

25. Tommy L. Bogger, *Free Blacks in Norfolk, Virginia, 1790–1860.* Charlottesville: University Press of Virginia, 1997, pp. 73–74.

26. Quoted in Phillips, *Freedom's Port*, p. 197.

27. Quoted in Berlin, *Slaves Without Masters*, p. 253.

28. Quoted in Berlin, *Slaves Without Masters*, p. 110.

Chapter 3:
Out on the Western Frontier

29. Quoted in William Loren Katz, *The Black West.* Garden City, NY: Doubleday, 1971, p. 4.

30. Quoted in Katz, *The Black West*, p. 24.

31. Quoted in Katz, *The Black West*, p. 32.

32. Quoted in Malcolm J. Rohrbough, *Days of Gold.* Berkeley and Los Angeles: University of California Press, 1997, p. 24.

33. Kenneth G. Goode, *California's Black Pioneers.* Santa Barbara, CA: McNally & Loftin, 1974, p. 59.

34. Quoted in Bracey, Meier, and Rudwick, *Free Blacks in America*, p. 117.

35. Quoted in Bracey, Meier, and Rudwick, *Free Blacks in America*, p. 117.

36. Quoted in Bracey, Meier, and Rudwick, *Free Blacks in America*, p. 118.

Chapter 4:
Serving Their Country

37. Washington, *The Story of the Negro*, p. 310.

38. Quoted in William C. Nell, *The Colored Patriots of the American Revolu-tion.* New York: Arno, 1968, pp. 16–17.

39. PBS, "Crispus Attucks c. 1723–1770," *Africans in America*, 1998. www.pbs.org/wgbh/aia/part2/2p24.html.

40. Quoted in Nell, *The Colored Patriots of the American Revolution*, p. 129.

41. Quoted in Ray Raphael, *A People's History of the American Revolution.* New York: New Press, 2001, p. 287.

42. Quoted in Paul Finkelman and Lorenzo J. Greene, *Slavery, Revolutionary America, and the New Nation.* New York: Garland, 1989, p. 243.

43. Finkelman and Greene, *Slavery, Revolutionary America, and the New Nation*, p. 244.

44. Quoted in Benjamin Quarles, *The Negro in the American Revolution.* Chapel Hill: University of North Carolina Press, 1966, p. 74.

45. Gerard T. Altoff, *Among My Best Men: African Americans and the War of 1812.* Put-in-Bay, OH: Perry Group, 1996, p. 11.

46. Quoted in Altoff, *Among My Best Men*, p. 40.

47. Quoted in Berlin, *Slaves Without Masters*, p. 126.

48. Quoted in Roland C. McConnel, *Negro Troops of Antebellum Louisiana.* Baton Rouge: Louisiana State University Press, 1968, p. 88.

49. Quoted in Office of the Secretary of Defense, "Black Americans in Defense of Our Nation," Maxwell-Gunter AFB, April 17, 1990. www.au.af.mil/au/awc/awcgate/usmchist/defense.txt.

50. Quoted in Washington, *The Story of the Negro*, p. 323.

51. Quoted in Washington, *The Story of the Negro*, pp. 329–30.

52. Washington, *The Story of the Negro*, p. 332.

Chapter 5: Intellectuals, Inventors, and Innovators

53. Portia P. James, *The Real McCoy: African-American Inventors and Innovation, 1619–1930*. Washington, DC: Smithsonian Institution Press, 1989, p. 23.

54. Edward Sidney Jenkins, *To Fathom More*. Lanham, MD: University Press of America, 1996, p. 8.

55. Quoted in Jenkins, *To Fathom More*, p. 5.

56. Quoted in Jenkins, *To Fathom More*, p. 11.

57. James, *The Real McCoy*, p. 30.

58. James, *The Real McCoy*, p. 30.

59. Quoted in James Oliver Horton and Lois E. Horton, *In Hope of Liberty*. New York: Oxford University Press, 1997, p. 58.

60. PBS, "The Forten Women, 1805–1883," *Africans in America*, 1998. www.pbs.org/wgbh/aia/part3/3p477.html.

61. James Michael Brodie, *Created Equal: The Lives and Ideas of Black American Innovators*. New York: William Morrow, 1993, p. 43.

62. Quoted in Jean M. West, "From a Sugar Bowl to the International Space Station: Norbert Rillieux, African-American Inventor," *Slavery in America*, 2004. www.slaveryinamerica.org/narratives/bio_norbert_rillieux.htm.

63. Quoted in James, *The Real McCoy*, p. 43.

64. James, *The Real McCoy*, p. 45.

Chapter 6: Fighting Slavery in Word and Deed

65. Quoted in University of Houston, "Antislavery: The Rise of Antislavery Thought," 2003. www.hfac.uh.edu/gl/antisl2.htm.

66. Quoted in Henrietta Buckmaster, *Let My People Go*. Boston: Beacon, 1966, p. 19.

67. Quoted in Leon F. Litwack, *North of Slavery*. Chicago: University of Chicago Press, 1961, p. 217.

68. Quoted in Litwack, *North of Slavery*, p. 226.

69. Quoted in Litwack, *North of Slavery*, p. 227.

70. Quoted in Bella Gross, *Clarion Call*. New York: Bella Gross, 1947, p. 1.

71. Gross, *Clarion Call*, p. 4.

72. Quoted in Gross, *Clarion Call*, p. 8.

73. Gross, *Clarion Call*, p. 16.

74. Gross, *Clarion Call*, p. 18.

75. Frederick Douglass, *My Bondage and My Freedom*. New York: Arno, 1968, p. 369.

76. Quoted in Litwack, *North of Slavery*, p. 225.

For Further Reading

Frederick Douglass, *My Bondage and My Freedom*. New York: Arno, 1968. First printed in 1845, this is the autobiography of the leading black abolitionist, detailing the hideous institution of slavery in poetic and emotionally charged language.

Bonnie Hinman, *Benjamin Banneker: American Mathematician and Astronomer.* Philadelphia: Chelsea House, 2000. A biography of the eighteenth-century African American who taught himself mathematics and astronomy and helped survey what would become Washington, D.C.

Portia P. James, *The Real McCoy: African-American Inventors and Innovation, 1619–1930*. Washington, DC: Smithsonian Institution Press, 1989. Explores the struggles and triumphs of black inventors as they changed the world while fighting against racial prejudice and oppression.

Media Project Inc., *Student Almanac of African American History*. Vol. 1: *From Slavery to Freedom, 1492–1876*. Westport, CT: Greenwood, 2003. A basic overview of the history of African Americans in the United States, with important figures, terms, timelines, maps, and source documents.

Philip Wolny, *The Underground Railroad: A Primary Source History of the Journey to Freedom*. New York: Rosen, 2004. Examines the events and key figures behind the formation and operation of the Underground Railroad, the secretive and illegal organization that helped American slaves escape to freedom in the northern United States and Canada.

Web Sites

The African American Mosaic
(www.loc.gov/exhibits/african/afam001.html). A sixteen-part Web site hosted by the Library of Congress with excerpts from rare books that focused on colonization of free blacks, black abolitionism, and other subjects.

Africans in America
(www.pbs.org/wgbh/aia/home.html). The companion Web site for the PBS television documentary that presents the journey of black people through slavery in four parts with slave narratives, photos, and resource links.

Free Blacks in the Antebellum Period
(http://lcweb2.loc.gov/ammem/aao html/exhibit/aopart2.html). A Web site that includes historical quotes from books by free blacks, along with reproductions of documents such as certificates of freedom that proved the nonslave status of holders.

Works Consulted

Books

Gerard T. Altoff, *Among My Best Men: African Americans and the War of 1812.* Put-in-Bay, OH: Perry Group, 1996. Black men were sailors and whalers on the Great Lakes in the early nineteenth century. This book tells of their service in the war between the United States and Great Britain.

Ira Berlin, *Slaves Without Masters.* New York: Pantheon, 1974. A well-written and thorough study of free blacks in the antebellum South that examines economics, white attitudes toward freemen, and population statistics.

Tommy L. Bogger, *Free Blacks in Norfolk, Virginia, 1790–1860.* Charlottesville: University Press of Virginia, 1997. Focuses on the lives of free blacks in a relatively small city, including their social status, occupations, landownership, and education.

John H. Bracey Jr., August Meier, and Elliot Rudwick, eds., *Free Blacks in America, 1800–1860.* Belmont, CA: Wadsworth, 1971. A collection of essays concerning life for free blacks in the nineteenth century with commentary on life in the South, North, and West.

James Michael Brodie, *Created Equal: The Lives and Ideas of Black American Innovators.* New York: William Morrow, 1993. The accomplishments of slave inventors, eighteenth-century freemen innovators, and the black men and women of the twentieth century who changed society with their mechanical knowledge and scientific understanding.

Henrietta Buckmaster, *Let My People Go.* Boston: Beacon, 1966. First published in 1941 by a Quaker author, this book examines the Underground Railroad, the abolition movement, and black struggles against racism, highlighting the roles performed by women.

John M. Duncan, *Travels Through Part of the United States and Canada in 1818 and 1819, Volume 1.* London: Hurst, Robinson, 1823. Observations of a Scottish traveler in North America in the early nineteenth century when the population of free blacks was increasing.

Paul Finkelman, ed., *Free Blacks in a Slave Society.* New York: Garland, 1989. Part of an eighteen-book series, this volume contains articles written throughout the twentieth century by historians who studied the lives and cultures of free blacks in Georgia, North Carolina, Delaware, and elsewhere.

Paul Finkelman and Lorenzo J. Greene, *Slavery, Revolutionary America, and the New Nation.* New York: Garland, 1989. Contains several dozen articles taken from books and magazines about blacks' participation in the Revolutionary War, largely written by leading historians.

John Hope Franklin, *The Free Negro in North Carolina, 1790–1860*. New York: W.W. Norton, 1971. First published in 1943, this study examines the demographics, legal status, economic standing, and social life of the free black population in North Carolina before the Civil War.

Kenneth G. Goode, *California's Black Pioneers*. Santa Barbara, CA: McNally & Loftin, 1974. The history of African Americans in California from the Spanish era in the 1700s through the second half of the twentieth century.

Bella Gross, *Clarion Call*. New York: Bella Gross, 1947. A history of the free black convention movement responsible for large abolitionist meetings that agitated against slavery in the South and repression in the North between the years 1817 and 1865.

James Oliver Horton and Lois E. Horton, *Black Bostonians*. New York: Holmes & Meier, 1979. A narrative of family life and community struggle in free black Boston during the antebellum period, when workers, abolitionists, and business owners worked and organized for mutual aid.

———, *In Hope of Liberty*. New York: Oxford University Press, 1997. A scholarly work that examines free blacks, slavery, urban life, revolution, abolition, and culture, race, and class in the colonial North.

William Jay and James Freeman Clarke, *The Free People of Color*. New York: Arno and New York Times, 1969. Two abolitionist essays concerning the plight of free blacks in nineteenth-century America. Jay's was written in 1838 and Clarke's in 1859.

Edward Sidney Jenkins, *To Fathom More*. Lanham, MD: University Press of America, 1996. Biographies of African American scientists and inventors from the eighteenth century to the 1990s.

William Loren Katz, *The Black West*. Garden City, NY: Doubleday, 1971. A study of western black explorers, fur traders, early settlers, cowboys, homesteaders, soldiers, and abolitionists.

Leon F. Litwack, *North of Slavery*. Chicago: University of Chicago Press, 1961. An examination of free black culture, politics, educational opportunities, religion, and abolitionism in the cities of the North during the antebellum period.

Roland C. McConnel, *Negro Troops of Antebellum Louisiana*. Baton Rouge: Louisiana State University Press, 1968. The story of the unique Battalion of Free Men of Color, which played an important role in military history between 1729 and the 1860s.

William C. Nell, *The Colored Patriots of the American Revolution*. New York: Arno, 1968. A book first published in 1855 that uses government documents, old newspaper articles, and interviews with elderly slaves to establish the fact that African Americans played an important part in the Revolution.

Jane H. Pease and William H. Pease, *They Who Would Be Free: Blacks' Search for Freedom, 1830–1861.* New York: Atheneum, 1974. An analysis of the perceptions, goals, attitudes, values, and means of northern free blacks who fought in the abolitionist crusade.

Christopher Phillips, *Freedom's Port.* Urbana: University of Illinois Press, 1997. A study of the free African American community in Baltimore between 1790 and 1860, focusing on the social circumstances and cultural development of the people.

Benjamin Quarles, *The Negro in the American Revolution.* Chapel Hill: University of North Carolina Press, 1966. The definitive book about blacks and their role in the American Revolution.

Ray Raphael, *A People's History of the American Revolution.* New York: New Press, 2001. A provocative and highly entertaining telling of the Revolution through the eyes of "real people," including working-class rebels, women, pacifists, Native Americans, and others, based on diaries, personal letters, and other eyewitness accounts.

Malcolm J. Rohrbough, *Days of Gold.* Berkeley and Los Angeles: University of California Press, 1997. A well-researched history of the California gold rush.

W. Sherman Savage, *Blacks in the West.* Westport, CT: Greenwood, 1976. A book that discusses the roles African Americans played in western migration, including slavery issues, military conquest, business growth, politics, and education.

Emma Lou Thornbrough, *The Negro in Indiana.* Indianapolis: Indiana Historical Bureau, 1957. Describes the population, economic situation, and culture of black residents of Indiana during the nineteenth century.

Booker T. Washington, *The Story of the Negro, Volume 1.* London: T. Fisher Unwin, 1909. The story of black people in Africa and as slaves in America, written by the renowned educator who founded the Tuskegee Institute, a college for blacks in Alabama.

Writers Program of the Work Projects Administration in the State of Virginia, *The Negro in Virginia.* New York: Hastings House, 1940. A study of the history of blacks in Virginia from their first arrival in the seventeenth century through the years of slavery and the years following the Civil War.

R.J. Young, *Antebellum Black Activists.* New York: Garland, 1996. A study of African American experiences, including fighting slavery, women abolitionists, society's view of black abolitionists, and the success of black antislavery conventions.

Internet Sources

Frederick Douglass, "Men of Color, to Arms!" March 21, 1863. Teaching AmericanHistory.org. http://teaching americanhistory.org/library/index.asp? document=440.

Horry County Historical Society, "Timber and Turpentine Industries," April 23, 1999. www.hchsonline.org/places/tur pentine.html.

Nathan Johnson, "Reason," The History of Mathematics, 2002. http://vulpix.netfirms.com/history/reason.html.

Office of the Secretary of Defense, "Black Americans in Defense of Our Nation," Maxwell-Gunter AFB, April 17, 1990. www.au.af.mil/au/awc/awcgate/usmchist/defense.txt.

PBS, "Crispus Attucks c. 1723–1770," *Africans in America*, 1998. www.pbs.org/wgbh/aia/part2/2p24.html.

———, "The Forten Women, 1805–1883," *Africans in America*, 1998. www.pbs.org/wgbh/aia/part3/3p477.html.

University of Houston, "Antislavery: The Rise of Antislavery Thought," 2003. www.hfac.uh.edu/gl/antisl2.htm.

Jean M. West, "From a Sugar Bowl to the International Space Station: Norbert Rillieux, African-American Inventor," Slavery in America, 2004. www.slaveryinamerica.org/narratives/bio_norbert_rillieux.htm.

Index

Picture Credits

Cover, Art Resource,N.Y.
Courtesy of Berkeley Museum, University of California, 50 (both)
© Bettmann/CORBIS, 3, 6, 13, 14, 27, 28-29, 36, 38, 42, 56, 63, 69, 75, 82, 93, 96
© Corbis, 10, 16, 22, 25, 32, 53, 57
Courtesy of The Denver Public Library, 47
Getty Images, 7, 43, 70
Hulton Archive/Getty Images, 83
Library of Congress, 76, 91
North Wind Picture Archives, 21, 87, 95
Picture History, 59

About the Author

Stuart A. Kallen is the author of more than two hundred nonfiction books for children and young adults. He has written on topics ranging from the theory of relativity to the history of rock and roll. In addition, Mr. Kallen has written award-winning children's videos and television scripts. In his spare time, Stuart A. Kallen is a singer/songwriter/guitarist in San Diego, California.